OTHER BOOKS BY SARAH YORK

Into the Wilderness

REMEMBERING
WELL

REMEMBERING WELL

RITUALS FOR CELEBRATING LIFE
AND MOURNING DEATH

SARAH YORK

JOSSEY-BASS
A Wiley Company
San Francisco

Jossey-Bass Inc., 350 Sansome Street, San Francisco, California 94104. Jossey-Bass is a registered trademark of Jossey-Bass Inc., A Wiley Company.

Jossey-Bass books and products are available through most bookstores. To contact Jossey-Bass directly, call (888) 378-2537, fax to (800) 605-2665, or visit our website at www.josseybass.com.
Substantial discounts on bulk quantities of Jossey-Bass books are available to corporations, professional associations, and other organizations. For details and discount information, contact the special sales department at Jossey-Bass.

Manufactured in the United States of America.

Library of Congress Cataloging-in-Publication Data

York, Sarah, date
    Remembering well : rituals for celebrating life and mourning death / Sarah York. —1st ed.
        p. cm.
    Includes bibliographical references and index.
    ISBN 0–7879–5507–8 (alk. paper)
    1. Memorial service. I. Title.
    BV199.M4 Y67 2000
    291.3'8—dc21
                                                                                  00-09231

FIRST EDITION
HB Printing   10 9 8 7 6 5 4 3 2 1

CONTENTS

PREFACE

MY MOTHER DIED IN APRIL 1983 IN HER HOME IN THE MOUNTAINS OF NORTH Carolina. She didn't want a funeral. "Get together and have a party," she had said when the topic was allowed to come up. This life is all there is as far as she was concerned, and when it's over, it's over—the less fuss the better.

We did not honor her request. We needed the ritual. We needed to say good-bye, but we also needed a ritual that would honor her spirit and would be faithful to her values and beliefs. She was hostile toward any expression of organized religion, so even though I was a minister, holding a memorial service in a church was out of the question.

Our task was to put together something that would honor and celebrate the life and spirit of this complex woman. My mother was a concert pianist, sculptor, equestrian, wife, and parent. She read at least one book a day, pieced quilts, milked cows, made cheese, built a log cabin (the old way), took in stray dogs, and wrote angry letters to her congressman and the IRS. Her best friends were college professors and toothless farmers, and she was equally at ease with either, hungry for the poetry of philosophy, art, and music as well as the poetry of the land.

She was full of contradictions: a naturalist who smoked too much, an atheist who knew the Bible better than most Christians. She was a sculptor whose most joy-filled work was chiseled out of the most painful depths of her soul. Generous and warm, she was also often depressed and self-abusive. Caring of others, she did not care enough for herself. A heavy smoker from the time she was thirteen, she died of emphysema. An alcoholic who could will herself sober for years, she was too proud to turn to AA or counseling when her will failed her. She was easy to love and hard to live with.

My father had made arrangements for cremation and a private service but wanted to give the neighbors in their small rural community an opportunity to "pay their respects." An evening visitation with a viewing of an open casket, the typical ritual in western North Carolina, was not appropriate. My father, an atheist who would never run his lawn mower on Sunday out of respect for his Baptist neighbors, did not want to offend them. So he rented an empty casket for the visitation in the funeral home and topped it with a beautiful spray of yellow roses. Neighbors filed by the closed casket, some of them touching it. One man knelt before the casket to offer a prayer.

On my mother's funeral day, we awakened to a clear, sun-filled spring morning, and the family walked the land to select a burial site for the ashes (legal in North Carolina). We were all drawn to the pond where she had built a waterfall and had planted azaleas, narcissus, willows, water lilies, and spring bulbs. She had called it her laughing place. Each of us took our turn with the shovel and lovingly cleared an area for people to stand. On a rock just above the site, we placed a large unfinished sculpture she had chiseled from a tree root that was smooth and worn from years of river life. Then we prepared the house for a small gathering of family and friends, placing flowers and some of her sculpture along the deck rail outside and more sculptures inside.

The simple service consisted of music and sharing. Knowing that my role was as daughter, not minister, I asked a dear friend to lead the service—giving it some form and setting a tone for our sharing. We laughed and cried through memory, pausing to pet the dogs that wandered among us. Most of those present told stories from their experiences with my mother. One person recalled the time when she encountered my mother planting peas in February and questioned her about planting so early. My mother the atheist dug her fingers into the thawing dirt and said, "You don't want to miss out on the resurrection, do you?" Another friend remembered the first time he met her. Without any sort of greeting, she leaned on the fence, chin resting on folded arms and cigarette hanging from the side of her mouth, looked him in the eye, and said, "What do you know about Spinoza?"

Most of the stories told were of her brilliance, her creativity, her humor, and her warmth. Several anecdotes involved animals she had rescued and nursed back to health, like Sam the stray hound, whose mangy smell was repulsive enough to make you gag, and Kleine, the neglected Doberman puppy spindly with rickets.

We briefly acknowledged my mother's tendency toward self-abuse, and that was enough. We did not need to dwell on it. To ignore it, however, would have been to ignore a significant aspect of who she was. Her parents had abandoned her, and she carried the scars of early wounds throughout her life. Her pain had also given her compassion and had shaped her wonderful sense of humor.

After the service, everyone was invited to take a flower (from a large vase in which we had put yellow roses from the casket spray and flowers from my mother's garden) and create a procession down the road to the burial site. There a close friend of my mother's read a poem she had written to her a few years before. My older brother poured the ashes into the ground, and I read some words I had written early that morning—some honest things I needed to say to her at that moment. We each placed our flowers in the ground and sprinkled a handful of earth into the grave. Our benediction was a recording of the opening fugue of the Beethoven String Quartet in C sharp Minor—my mother's favorite piece. As others moved back up the hill to share the wonderful bounty of food that had been brought by friends and neighbors, a few of us lingered to finish filling in the grave. My younger brother brought out some crocus bulbs, and we planted them around the site. "You don't plant bulbs in the spring," I thought. Then I smiled. "Well, you don't want to miss out on the resurrection, do you?"

When I walked back up the hill, I hurt. But I felt good, because I had not let anyone protect me or my family from our grief. I had asked each of my mother's closest friends to do something—lead the service, play the piano, share a poem, preserve the tree-root sculpture for outdoor life—knowing that they needed to participate in ways that helped them express their love and loss.

When my father died three years later, we shaped a very different kind of memorial. He was a well-known cartoonist, a person with a public following. So symbiotic was he with the characters in his *Gasoline Alley* comic strip that any memorial for him would have to include strangers who ingested the gentle humor of Walt Wallet and his family with their morning coffee. To conduct the service, then, we asked the minister at the local Unitarian Universalist church to be in charge. Although he was familiar with my father's work, he had not known my father personally, so we spent an hour or so sharing our stories of my father's gentle and humble spirit. We spoke of his devotion to family and of the loneliness he had suffered since the deaths of my mother and younger brother (who died six months before my father). We sketched word pictures of Daddy bent over his drawing board, sucking away at the ever-present pipe, wearing old worn sweaters with holes where tobacco embers had dropped and others of Daddy working in his small, cluttered studio, listening to a baseball game on the radio while watching another on the television. We evoked memories of simple pleasures and smiled as we pictured him walking through the pasture, long white hair blowing, his five large dogs running, sniffing, and exploring. The minister would not need to use all of this in his remarks; it was just therapeutic for us to offer up our love as we wandered through years of memory.

We had selected speakers for the service, and we wanted people to have an opportunity to share brief memories or images in an informal, spontaneous way. We put together a service folder with one of his drawings on the back. Just as the earthy, informal living room service was right for my mother, so this more traditional gathering was right for my father. I chose not to speak at his service.

After a reception at the church, we returned to the homestead to commit his ashes to the land. You might expect that we would place his ashes with those of his wife and son. With half of them, that is what we did. He liked to hike high up on the hill behind his house, stopping off along the way at a couple of "resting places." So our silent procession of family and close friends followed his favorite trail, with the dogs, as usual, trotting along. We distributed the remainder of his ashes on the path and at the highest resting place.

"Give sorrow words," wrote Shakespeare in the tragedy of *Macbeth*, "The grief that does not speak / Whispers the o'erfraught heart and bids it break."

At no time are these words more poignant than when we honor and bury the dead. As a person who has grieved and as a minister who has been there with others in their grief, I have learned that current practices often deny death and protect us from the pain of grief. The grief that does not "speak" in some way— through crying or talking or ritual activity; through tributes of charity or creative expression—remains unresolved. And what a powerful and destructive force it has for years to come!

Most of us, however, are uncomfortable with deep and strong emotions—fearful of getting out of control. Physicians will prescribe tranquilizers, for example, to help someone get through the first days or weeks after a death. Years later, when repressed grief causes depression, they prescribe antidepressant drugs to mask the feelings.

Though it is impossible to make a general statement that applies to all people, it is safe to say that grief issues are more destructive to a person when they are suppressed or repressed than when they are expressed.

But how does one go about expressing deep sorrow, anger, or guilt? These are private feelings, layered with years of relationship and charged with unpredictable emotional turmoil. It is in the midst of loss and grief that each of us is most vulnerable. It is our natural impulse to avoid circumstances that evoke our strong or uncontrolled emotions.

For centuries, religious traditions have provided a safe place for the expression of feelings through ritual. In the decades leading up to the twenty-first century, however, we have witnessed, particularly among individuals born after World War II, an alienation and exodus from traditional religion. This has given rise to an increasing number of people for whom traditional religious ritual has become empty, awkward, or irrelevant.

This book is written for anyone who has ever or will ever suffer through the death of someone they loved. This includes those who wish to give new meaning to the time-honored rituals of their faith as well as those who have broken with tradition.

Some people who do not have a religious affiliation are fortunate enough to find clergy who work with them to create ceremonies that are comfortable and appropriate. In increasing numbers, others plan their own services, usually creating a secular gathering to share memories and privately scattering or burying cremated remains.

Too many, however, choose to have no service or committal ceremony at all. An urn containing the ashes of a man's wife may sit on the mantelpiece of his home for years after her death. The body of a child born dead may be left in the hospital for disposal. A widow may scatter the ashes of her husband in a silent and solitary gesture, depriving her children and others close to him of the opportunity for closure.

Even in circumstances such as these, rituals can be devised to offer healing and encourage a healthy process through the stages of grief. Whether a ceremony takes place a few days after a death or several years later, it can be designed to address issues of loss that linger unresolved. It can also offer spiritual meaning without a religious context.

Shakespeare, who urged readers to "give sorrow words," also spoke of the inevitability of death. "The readiness is all," he wrote in the tragedy *Hamlet*. He spoke, of course, of a readiness of the mind and spirit. Whether you are planning for a recent death or preparing yourself for the time when your own body gives out, it is my hope that the stories, examples, and guidelines provided in this book will assist you with the readiness of your mind and spirit for life's final rites of passage.

Although readers will derive the most benefit by reading the text in its entirety, the book is designed so that those who have a specific and urgent need for help with planning a memorial ceremony can find what they need without having to read every page. The book is not written like a textbook. Its stories of love and loss, tenderness and tension may evoke painful thoughts and memories or stir chords of grief and compassion. Please care for yourself as you read, and pace yourself if it becomes too difficult to read the entire book all at once.

Chapter One addresses the discomfort many people experience when they consider creating and conducting a service. It describes some of the first services I conducted and relates how families helped me become more comfortable with my role.

Chapter Two presents practical guidelines for planning a memorial service, offering a rationale for each element of the service, suggestions for creating a rhythm or style that suits the occasion, and examples of phrases that can be used to open or close a service or introduce a time of shared remembrance.

Chapter Three discusses the functions of prayer and prayerful gestures such as lighting candles and emphasizes the spiritual context for remembering well.

Chapter Four deals with some of the difficult decisions that have to be made when a death occurs. Since many of these decisions have to be made immediately in the midst of grief, I recommend reading it when there is not a pressing need to do so—like right now.

In Chapter Five, I discuss my approach to interviewing families and writing a "soul sketch" or memorial portrait of a person who has died. This chapter will be especially useful to professionals such as clergy or therapists who will be in the position of helping family and friends plan for a memorial service.

Chapter Six covers the need to fashion ritual expression that addresses the circumstances of death, such as terminal illness, suicide, murder, or an accident.

Chapter Seven approaches the sensitive topic of family alienation. There is seldom a death that does not bring together people in varying degrees of tension with one another or with the person they gather to remember. Although a memorial ritual cannot bring about instant reconciliation, there is a power in the holy intimacy of this time of vulnerability and grief that can be used to hold up images of healing, forgiveness, and hope.

Chapter Eight discusses committal ceremonies. In some cases, a committal (a ceremony to bury a body or distribute cremated remains) occurs right after a memorial service. Increasingly, however, families plan a separate ceremony, often taking cremated remains to a special place and holding a private gathering.

Chapter Nine, recognizing that grief does not end with a memorial service, invites the reader to create rituals through the seasons of grief, particularly during the first year. This chapter then suggests examples of ritual expression that assist those who carry the wounds of grief as they deal with unresolved issues such as guilt or anger.

In addition to an annotated list of recommended reading, there are three resources. Resource One offers rituals of blessing and preparing a body for burial or cremation. Resource Two includes examples of services created by families or communities who sought little or no participation of clergy. Resource Three provides readings, prayers, and blessings for use in services or ceremonies. (Further resources are listed at my web site, www.sarahyork.com.)

It would be impossible to write this book without using examples from experience. Many people have offered their stories with delight, and those people are identified by name. Others are represented in composite examples. In order to offer the most useful information and protect the privacy of people who have trusted me with their most vulnerable feelings, I have intentionally altered not only names but also many of the details of particular cases. In some instances, even where services were public and the information I share was offered in the public domain, I have changed names and some of the details for the sake of assuring the privacy of the people involved.

June 2000   Sarah York
Fairview, North Carolina

For Chuck

and in grateful memory of my mother,
Gretchen Cora Moores
(1917–1983)

and my father,
Richard A. Moores
(1909–1986)

GRATITUDES

A MYSTERIOUS PACKAGE ARRIVED IN THE MAIL. OPENING THE PADDED ENVELOPE, I noted first that it contained several smooth stones engraved or embossed with words or Chinese characters. "Hope" and "Joy" were carved into two of them. The Chinese character for "Compassion" decorated another. On the fourth stone, a labyrinth was imprinted. This one, titled "Shepherd's Race," was described as an ancient and sacred pattern that invites preparation for a time of transformation.

A brief note explained that the stones were a gift. The man who designs and manufactures them had had three separate conversations with people who had recently attended a memorial service that I had conducted. He wanted to affirm the work I was doing.

The gift of stones was a grateful response from a stranger for a memorial service that he had not been able to attend. This gesture stimulated me to think about writing a book that would help others remember their friends and family members well. This book is an expression of my gratitude, inspired by the gratitude others have expressed to me.

It is my privilege as a Unitarian Universalist minister to be present with families for the joys and sorrows of their lives, and it has been a special privilege to create with them rites of passage at times of birth, marriage, and death. It is in creating rites of death in particular that I have experienced a bond of holy intimacy with the people who trust me with their grief. And I have learned so much from them. Represented in the pages of this volume are hundreds of people, living and dead, who taught me how to grieve and how to help others express their love and pain in ritual. To them I make my first offering of gratitude. In addition to many who are anonymous, I thank those who have honored the memory of their loved ones by sharing their stories: Ruth Codier Resch, Beth Allen, Michael Comando and Nanette True, Judy Cosdon, Julie Hatchard Dybdahl, Al Melkonian, Sue Broidy, Barbara Sims-Bell, Bradley Miles, Ginny Callaway and David Holt, Dennis Axelrod, Nancy and Christyn Edmundson, and Jere Jacob.

Several of my clergy colleagues shared examples from their experience. These include Maureen Killoran (my minister), Ken Collier, Laurel Hallman, Suzanne Meyer, Mary E. M. Moore, and Janet Harvey, as well as some whose readings are included in Resource Three. I also thank Rabbi Robert Ratner, who directed me to the resources of his tradition. Mark Belletini could have written this book himself, and I thank him for sharing his creative gifts and his own story.

Two gifted psychotherapists, Hendrika de Vries and Donna Clifton McGuire, shared the wisdom of their profession, drawing from their understanding of ritual, storytelling, and the spiritual dimensions of grief. I thank them both for their compassionate offerings.

My friends have been there for me from the beginning, willing to read rough drafts of proposals and manuscripts and gently encouraging me to forge ahead when I was discouraged. First among these is Eva Haller, who is second only to my husband, Chuck, when it comes to supporting me through the stages of getting this book out of my head and onto paper. Her wise and affectionate response to the news that I had a publisher was, "Oh, does that mean you have to *write* the book?" Janet Harvey has "been there" as always, with her personal support and her remarkable skills as a writer, mediator, hospital chaplain, and youth leader. Jerry Godard, who conducted my mother's memorial service and cried with me through several family deaths, has reviewed my writing with the wisdom of his heart along with that of his brilliant intellect.

Lee Blue and Steve Beall, whose red pens were informed by their personal experience and professional expertise, gently improved my prose, as did Ginny Callaway and Olivia Woodford from my writing group.

Jennifer Louden, who knows this writing and publishing business so well, has tutored me through the whole process, and Barbara Moulton was wonderfully available when I needed her counsel. Marcia Meier, Barbara Sims-Bell, Sylvia Ann Hewlett, and Armando Nieto, savvy writers all, also helped me launch this book.

My editor, Sheryl Fullerton, has shared my vision for this book from the beginning, and her enthusiasm for the project has been an inspiration. In addition to being a superb professional with spiritual depth as well as good judgment, she is one wonderful person to work with. Joanne Clapp Fullagar has overseen the production process with remarkable skill, patience, and sensitivity. In fact, everyone at Jossey-Bass who has worked with me on this book seems to share a sense of mission about publishing. They understand that what they are doing will make a difference in the lives of their readers and in our world.

Chuck Campbell is my beloved husband and best friend, and he knows when I need a supportive word or a gentle prod. The first one to read the book in the rough, he helped me smooth it out. In deep and abiding gratitude, I have dedicated this book to him, and to the memory of my parents, who are lovingly present with me every day.

REMEMBERING
WELL

CHAPTER ONE

Giving Sorrow Words

Families and Funerals

I FREQUENTLY SPEAK WITH PEOPLE WHO SAY THEY DO NOT WANT ANY SERVICES held when they die. One woman in her nineties told me just after attending a service for a friend, "That was really a nice service, Sarah, but I'm not going to have one of those when I die."

I smiled as I replied, "Eunice, you won't be in a position to have much to say about that."

I went on to tell her that her family would need it and so would many of us in the congregation, and we would want to hold a service. She and I have both affectionately retold the story of this conversation—she to reaffirm her initial desire in spite of what others do, and I to make the point that the ritual is not for her but for those who love her, will miss her, and must go on living without her.

Eunice says that she just doesn't want anyone to make a fuss over her, and she means it. I believe that most people who choose to avoid ritual, however, do so for one of two reasons. Either they do not want to deal with the emotions that are evoked by death, or they cannot conceive of such a ritual apart from a traditional religious context that is not relevant for them. In some cases, they may be very private individuals who have never liked the idea of having people talk about them "behind their back."

Whatever the reasons, they are not sufficient. *No exceptions. No matter what the circumstances of a life or a death, there is no reason not to mark the occasion of death with at least a simple private ceremony.* Thus it is that I always counsel families to consider, with love, other ways to respect the intent of those who have requested "no services." Then we work to create a ceremony that will honor the person who died while giving the family an opportunity to celebrate a life and mourn a death.

"Give sorrow words," Shakespeare admonished. But how do you begin to think about planning for a ritual if you have no religious tradition or perhaps even a distaste for ritual in general? If you are alienated from your faith tradition, how do you draw what is still meaningful from it and include it in a personalized ritual? How do you create an appropriate context to "give sorrow words"? The thought of taking on such a task is daunting enough. Add to that the fact that many deaths occur suddenly and without warning, requiring that some of the arrangements be made within a matter of days.

The fear of taking on the responsibility for a ritual of death may be the greatest of all obstacles to be overcome. The best way to overcome the fear, however, is to do it, finding others who will help. Your confidence comes as you realize that others have done this and you can, too. In Chapter Two, I will offer suggestions for involving friends or professionals in your planning.

Although I am writing after nearly two decades of planning and conducting memorial services and funerals, I can remember well when I did this for the very first time. I was a second-year student in divinity school, working as an intern in a local congregation. The minister who was my supervisor and mentor was on vacation. We had not yet had the opportunity for training in this matter of planning a memorial.

Death, however, has no regard for clergy vacation schedules. Ruth Codier had completed eighty years of living and died at home without warning. It was her daughter, Ruth Resch, who called, shaken by her mother's sudden death. Having arrived from out of town, she was planning to go to the funeral home to make arrangements.

I felt entirely inadequate. I wanted to tell her to call someone else—like a "real" minister. But I was being asked to stand in for Ruth's beloved minister. If I really wanted to pursue this calling, I would have to face up to doing a death ritual on my own for the first time. To add to my discomfort, Ruth had been a somewhat crusty woman, and I had not gotten to know her well.

I offered to accompany Ruth's daughter to the funeral home, and she accepted gratefully. I had no idea how important an offer that would turn out to be.

In accordance with both her mother's wishes and her own preference, Ruth's daughter requested that her mother's body be cremated. But I could tell she had some uncertainty about the decision.

In the presence of the funeral director, I asked her if she wished to see the body first. Yes, she did. The funeral official explained that without cosmetic preparations, Ruth did not look so good, and the daughter might want to reconsider. Her daughter just needed to see the reality of her mother's death, not "prettied up," and to say goodbye to the physical body of her mother. Reluctantly, the funeral director complied and asked for a few moments to make Ruth more presentable. As it turned out, Ruth did not look bad. She just looked dead, and that was part of what her daughter needed to take in. Her mother was gone. She would not have another conversation with the woman. She would not see her mother again—ever.

I was asked to plan a simple service for interring the ashes at the cemetery. (A memorial service would be held when Ruth's minister returned.) Ruth's daughter, a psychotherapist, and her granddaughter Rachel, met with me to plan. They knew they wanted to participate in the ceremony and to offer opportunities for others as well. After a series of long-distance calls, we pulled together what they wanted, drawing from their memories of Ruth's wishes.

At the service, we walked slowly from the cars to a cemetery site where we were shaded from the summer sun by a beautiful fir tree. I offered a brief introduction, then Ruth's daughter greeted those who gathered. Ruth's granddaughter read a selection about the meaning of death (a reading that Ruth had requested), Ruth's son read a selection from his Episcopalian liturgy, and I followed their readings with a brief spoken meditation. Before pouring her mother's ashes in the ground, Ruth's daughter read a poem her mother had written, titled "To Morning":

> When I go out my door I breathe the air
> And know the freshness and the newness there.
> Behind are left the endless small concerns
> The petty matters that consume and burn.
> My morning speaks and sparkles
>   When I go out my door.
> One fine gay day my morning does not wait
> for me to leave my airless room.
> But trim and debonair he makes an entrance.
> I do not rack and rage against the dark.

My morning walks with me
   When I go out my door.

   Then Ruth's daughter knelt with the cremated remains of her mother and
said,

     Truly you were as you were . . . for each of us here.
     . . . Gutsy lady, rare independent spirit,
     Uncommonly capable of growth
     Demanding in friendship, but you gave equally to your friends.
     You had courage. Deep convictions.
     And you went much farther out on a limb in acting on your
        convictions than most of us.
     You were like a great vintage wine: the bite was harsh in the
        beginning,
     Your aging grew better and better,
     Your spirit kept growing fuller, and it was many faceted,
     Your bouquet was finally a big and full-bodied one, for us.
     I will say for each person here that you modeled something very
        deeply important for each of us . . . no doubt honed quite
        individually for each one.
     As your daughter, I finally feel unabashedly privileged to have
        had you as my mother.
     You have crossed the line exactly as you wanted to: gracefully
        and tactfully.
     You done it, ole girl!
     I grieve for you and I am happy for you.
     You have triumphed.
     Bless you.

So it is time now for it to be my privilege to give your body into
   this earth.

Ruth's daughter poured the ashes directly into the open fertile earth in silence. Then Rachel held a clay vessel over the ashes. It contained earth from
Ruth's birthplace (brought by Ruth only weeks before), some stones, and other
symbolic objects. She broke it onto the ashes and said, "The vessel is broken."
Ruth's daughter continued, saying, "Ashes to ashes, my dear, and dust to dust."

I invited friends and family to place flowers into the earth and to help cover
the ashes with dirt. The daughter planted a lovely geranium from her mother's
garden over them. As she did so, I spoke the following words:

> When Ruth spoke of death and of her own death, she said, "I have a kind of
> 'knowing' that life has continuity; an essence that isn't destroyable." She imaged
> this knowing in the continuity of nature, saying she would return in the flow-
> ers. This flowering plant from Ruth's garden affirms her knowing and ours.

I invited those gathered to exchange a silent greeting of support to one another—a reminder that we do not grieve alone—then offered some closing
comments:

> Ruth has gone out her door into the morning, crossing the threshold peace-
> fully, courageously, and triumphantly. As we move from this place of burial,
> we too cross a threshold. We move in sadness for our loss, but we carry with
> us Ruth's own triumph and an awareness that her greatest concerns were for
> the continuity of life: recycling resources, striving for world peace, preserving
> the natural world for future generations. It was characteristic of Ruth to say,
> when she completed something, "Well, now, that's all settled. Let's move on."
> We might well imagine that in her own gentle gruffness she speaks to us now,
> saying, "Carry on. Carry on."

We go out our door into the day. Let us walk into the day with knowledge of the night, and into night with knowledge of the dawn.

I had never conducted such a ceremony, and initially I felt entirely inadequate for the task, but together with Ruth's daughter and granddaughter, I facilitated a service that was powerful and meaningful. That's because we worked together. Most important, they created their own fitting ritual for this act of loving leave-taking.

I learned from them, too. I would not have thought to fill a vessel with earth from Ruth's birthplace and break it over the ashes. That was their contribution to ritual—a poignant and powerful gesture. Likewise the gesture of silent greeting and touching—a very moving and meditative interaction—was their idea.

Because this family took an active role in creating the rituals for this ceremony, it helped each of them through this initial transition and the first stages of grief. It was grief expressed, not grief suppressed.

The next opportunity for me to perform a memorial service was during my final year of divinity school. A young couple had tried for several years to have a second child, and had grieved through four miscarriages. Finally, Christine had carried a child to term. When she went to the hospital to give birth, the nursery had been decorated, the clothing purchased, the house made ready. The baby, however, whose heart was beating only minutes before birth, was born dead. She never took her first breath.

The parents, devastated by this cruel death, were not sure what they wanted to do. Here was a fully developed human being who never had a chance to live. Would they give her a name? Would they go through the ritual of a funeral?

I asked them to describe their loss to me. As they spoke, it was very clear that they had indeed lost a child and would give her a service of burial. They chose also to give her the name she had been called while she grew to term—Rebecca.

I met them at the funeral home and members of their families joined us, along with a few close friends. We followed the hearse to the cemetery, where Neil and his brother carried the small closed casket to the burial site. Just seeing the diminutive box that held the infant's tiny body moved me to tears.

As we gathered around the freshly dug grave overlooking a flowing river, I spoke:

> We have come here this afternoon to this place to commit the body of Neil and Christine's infant child Rebecca to the earth. This child did not have the opportunity to breathe, to laugh, or to cry. She was, however, nurtured through these months of fetal life, and with her Neil and Christine have nurtured their hopes for their life with her. We grieve for the life she did not have. We grieve for the life that Neil and Christine will not have with her.

Taking a handful of dirt and dropping it on the casket, I said,

> We commit Rebecca's body to the earth, and with her a rosebud.

The parents placed the rosebud on the casket, then I said,

> Although this life may not bloom, may the budding of possibility bring new life out of death.

I then offered the following prayer:

> We come before you, Spirit of life and death, in wonder, in humility, in anger, and in hope. Daily we are touched by the rhythms of life and death, yet now we are out of rhythm, for birth and death have seized upon the same moment.
>
> In sadness for the hopes that are lost, we ask for new hope.

While grieving for this child's lost life, we ask for renewal and new life. Still asking why this death occurred, we seek understanding and peace.

With gratitude for the strength and love that Christine and Neil have for each other and that (*names of family present*) have shared with them, we ask for continued strength and love. Amen.

The closing benediction was simple and traditional:

The peace that passes understanding—
    the peace of the Spirit
    which the world can neither give nor take away—
    be among us and abide in our hearts,
    now and always.
    Amen.

This ritual offered Christine and Neil an opportunity to grieve a deep loss that was not adequately acknowledged by many of their friends or associates. Some people had even tried to console them by saying how fortunate they were that they already had one child. But the ritual was an acknowledgment of their loss. This infant daughter who never breathed in this world grew through nine months of development, her heart beating with hope and promise.

Two times during the first months of my ministry I was asked to prepare a memorial, and each presented unique challenges. In both cases, the individuals died in their mid-forties. I had the added challenge of dealing with both memorials on the same day. Their juxtaposition provided an interesting contrast.

It is said that form follows function. In the case of ritual, form follows the personality, values, and life meanings of the person who is being remembered.

In one case, I conducted a graveside service for a man whose forty-five years of life had been devoted primarily to his professional life. He was quite a success in business, but by his own admission, he had given little of himself to relationships. He demanded of others what he demanded of himself—excellence in all things. He was a man of intelligence, integrity, and courage. The tone for his sparsely attended service was cool, dignified, and respectfully loving, which was appropriate for this man who made his mark on Madison Avenue and worked himself into an early grave. No one in the family wanted to participate, and his wife did not want to invite anyone to speak, so I offered some scripture and prayer and made brief comments about the man's life. I left with the feeling that we had performed the obligatory ritual, but much had been left unsaid. I suspect that the atmosphere of controlled emotion and careful speech reflected the tone of the relationships he had had in life.

Later the same day, hundreds of people poured into our little sanctuary to celebrate the life of a brilliant playwright and poet who had touched their lives with her wit, her passion, her depth, and her humor. The service, like her life, was charged with emotion, with love, with earthy humor, and with creative expression. I opened the service with these words:

Good afternoon, friends. On this chilly winter day, this space is made sacred with the warm spirit of love and caring. For we, the friends and family of Jane Chambers, have gathered to celebrate Jane's life, to hold her up in human memory and divine mystery, to mourn our loss and to say goodbye.

We've come here first to remember Jane—to remember her at her times of passionate and unrelenting strength and power as well as her times of deep and full depression or dependence; to remember her both as a free and untamed spirit and as a creative home-builder and nester; to remember her as she was at the front of the movement for women's rights, taking the blows for others, and as she was in her more vulnerable moments, relying on others to care for her.

We have come to remember.

We have come also to mourn—to mourn in the silent spaces she once filled with her expansive laughter; to mourn in the empty places she once filled with her commanding presence; to mourn for the loss of love growing into tomorrow, deepening and maturing more through years of joy and conflict; to mourn for the words she might have spoken or written.

Our tears of sadness for the loss of life, full and blossoming and beautiful, mingle with tears of sadness for the loss of possibilities yet to be met. We are here to mourn.

We are also here to grow through an ending into a beginning, to let go of Jane and, with memories gathered for the journey, gain strength for moving through the days ahead without her.

Jane wouldn't like that, of course—us going on without her. She wanted too, too much to be with us. She had more love to give, more causes to win, more plays to write, more living to do. She said as much in her play *Kudzu,* through old Ginger, who was "getting fixed to die." Ginger had this to say about dying: "Now don't you start in talking to me about salvation and letting Jesus take me to heaven, because I ain't ready to go yet."

Jane wasn't ready to go yet, and we weren't ready to let her go, but she has left us, and we pause here today to celebrate her life, to mourn her death, to let go of her, and to gain strength for meeting tomorrow.

I then invited the congregation to join in singing what Jane had called "that awful blackbird song" ("Morning Has Broken"), noting that Jane sometimes loved what she hated and hated what she loved.

With Jane's own words inviting affectionate laughter from the beginning, the remainder of the service was a celebration of Jane's life. Several of her friends and family offered tributes in music and poetry as well as personal testimony to ways she had enriched their lives. The service was followed by a traditional procession to the cemetery for burial.

The first ritual I performed for Jane, however, was not her funeral. Beth, Jane's life partner of fourteen years, called me on the morning of her death, and I went over to the house. Beth and a friend were there, and I asked if they would like to offer some words of blessing for Jane before her body was removed.

I do not remember what any of us said. I opened by saying that we gathered this last time at Jane's bedside to say good-bye and offer blessings for her spirit. The friend chose a reading from the Psalms. I suspect that I offered a prayer of gratitude that Jane, who had suffered deeply for several months of illness, was free of suffering and had been surrounded by love as she died in her own home amid family and friends. I suspect that Beth offered loving words of good-bye. What we said was not so important as making a space for an invitation to holy mystery in these awkward and painful moments before her body was taken from that bed where she had spent most of her final year of life.

We then went into another room as the professionals did their job. It made sense not to watch as the person who had been a beloved companion in life became a body being loaded onto a gurney.

In Resource One, there is a discussion of the use of ritual for family or friends who want to come together in a similar way before a body is removed from a home or a hospital room, along with suggestions for rituals such as washing or dressing a body for burial or cremation. Again, the level of participation is up to the family. It is easy for any family to gather in silence for a few moments, perhaps holding hands or touching the body together. Words are not necessary for a gesture to have meaning. It is also nonthreatening to have someone read a poem or a verse. Rituals involving more direct participation with a body or with cremated remains require a level of comfort that may be right for some members of a family and not for others.

What is important is to find the appropriate level of comfort and participate according to what feels right. Too often participation of family members is minimal. Opportunities for ritual that will help them grieve are missed. It is just easier to leave it up to the professionals—undertakers, ministers, health care workers—to take care of everything.

Most of what I know about how to create a memorial ritual I learned when I was thrown into the waters of that first year of ministry. When I suggest here that a person doesn't have to be a minister to do this, I am saying that this is the heart of life; it is where we all live. This is our spiritual work—to mark our losses and celebrate our love. It is not the work of funeral directors and ministers—it is the work of families and friends. We who are the professionals are there to assist them with their work. It is to people like Ruth's daughter and Jane's friends and family that I offer gratitude, because they have known that I am just there to help them do what they have to do.

Through the years, I have learned from many more families. Some of the rituals we devised grew quite naturally out of the rich soil of memory. Eleven grandchildren gathered at one memorial, and while the oldest grandchild read a poem and shared some memories, the other ten all lit candles. Another family provided flowers at the door of the sanctuary and invited everyone who entered to take a flower and put it in a large basket in the front, thus creating a community bouquet. At the end of the service, each person was invited to take a flower from the bouquet.

For a woman who had been devoted to world peace, the space was decorated with international flags.

For a man who died of AIDS, a beautifully crafted panel for the AIDS Memorial Quilt was on display. Candles were lit in memory of others who had died of AIDS.

For a woman who had been a poet, a booklet of her poetry was put together and offered to friends and family who came to the service.

For a woman who found meaning in Native American traditions, the service began with an invocation to the four directions and ended with a Native American benediction.

Form follows function. If we want to celebrate a life, the possibilities are endless.

Music, of course is a universal medium for ritual. Too many people neglect to participate in this aspect of a memorial and let a funeral home select music for them. My experience is that funeral directors will work with families to give them what they want. There is no reason for not taking an active role and selecting music that contributes to the mood and meaning of the service. Bach may be perfect for one person, the Grateful Dead for another.

Yes, this is the family's work. If a person thinks to leave behind some requests and instructions, that makes the family's work easier. A member of one congregation, for example, asked for several selections of Beatles music to be played at her service. She had written a poem to her family that she wanted me to read. She left the rest up to us.

If a person doesn't indicate any particular wishes, however, that makes the family's work more meaningful. It invites family members to talk about what they need to do and what is right. It invites them to participate—to give sorrow words and music and gesture.

As they participate, they remember.

As they remember, they grieve.

As they grieve, they love.

CHAPTER TWO

In Loving Memory

Composing a Service

THINK, FOR A MOMENT, ABOUT FUNERALS OR MEMORIAL SERVICES YOU have attended. First, think back to the ones that most helped you through your process of grieving. What parts were most healing for you? Second, think about the services that least met your needs. What was missing? What turned you off?

When I ask people in workshops to describe the services that have best met their needs, the first thing they say, almost without exception, is that they felt they were celebrating the person. They could feel his or her presence. Then they say the service left them with a feeling that they were able to begin letting go of the person who died. They were able to say good-bye and keep something of the person's essence in their heart. Regardless of their religious perspective, they experienced a sense of hope that comes through death. They were held in a space where they felt safe, where their feelings were named. They shared a sense of holy intimacy with others, even if they never spoke with one another.

When people are least served by a memorial service, it is almost always for one of two reasons. The most frequent response is that the service was too impersonal. The second most reiterated reason is that they could not relate to a religious perspective that emphasized life after death more than life before death or glossed over difficult or conflicted feelings with a too-easy message of eternal peace.

I am only guessing, but I suspect that the impersonal services were those where the persons conducting the services spent less than two hours meeting with family and friends to plan it.

A conference with family is the place to begin. If you are to officiate, conversations with intimates allow you to evaluate the needs these people will have when they attend the service. This is also the time to gather information needed to write a "soul sketch," a memorial portrait of the person who died. And other parts of the service must be planned as well. When speaking with family members, keep in mind that you will want to create a style or mood in keeping with the spirit of the person being remembered. Meet for a minimum of two hours, and take breaks as needed. If meeting in their home, ask that your time together not be interrupted by visits or phone calls.

WHO WILL CREATE AND CONDUCT THE SERVICE?

A few years ago, I received a call from a woman whose husband was diagnosed with terminal cancer. The couple had no religious community, and as they considered what kind of memorial they wanted to have, they knew they did not want a service in the context of religious beliefs that were not their own. A neighbor had referred them to me, and they invited me to lunch so that we could get acquainted. It was the first time I had been interviewed by people for the job of doing a memorial service. Whether or not they interviewed anyone else, I do not know.

Most people are not so direct in their approach to shopping for the person who will officiate at their memorial. But think about it. Before you choose someone to cut your hair, you want to know the haircutter will style it to your satisfaction. If the stylist only does short and curly and you want long and straight, it is best to know this before that person is standing over you with scissors in hand.

Similarly, it is best to know what kind of approach a person will take to leading a memorial before he or she takes microphone in hand. Those who give some attention to finding a religious professional who suits their needs will be better served than those who passively employ whoever is available without exploring the approach the person will take. Many clergy work with families to personalize services. Indeed, it is my hope that this book is of use to them and the families who create services with them.

A growing number of people, however, do not want any traditional religious context for their memorial. Instead of a religious professional, they want someone they know and trust to conduct the service. This was the case for a family from outside my congregation that contacted me with a different kind of request. They wanted the benefit of my experience but did not want me to preside at the memorial ceremony. Joni Axelrod was in the advanced stages of bone cancer. Her therapist, Donna McGuire, had been working with Joni, her family, and her friends as they went through the painful process of accepting and planning for her imminent death. Joni wanted Donna to conduct the ceremony. Donna was willing to do it, and she met with me as she planned for a meaningful service.

My role in a situation such as this becomes that of a consultant. More clergy may be asked to serve families in this way as the funeral industry goes through some radical changes. Some people, like Joni's family, have time to think about plans before death occurs. Others choose cremation and set the date for a memorial a few weeks or even months after the death in order to have time to plan for the event. Looking for alternatives to the traditional clergy-led memorial, many people are turning to counselors or friends to lead their services. Often these laypeople, schooled in the issues of grief, gifted as speakers, and skilled in the art of ritual or ceremony, are capable of helping families who do not choose to work with a religious professional. Some, like Donna McGuire, are grounded in a deep sense of spirituality and bring their gift of faith to their work.

Some families are able to plan and conduct the service without any assistance. These are rare. In most cases, people are rendered so vulnerable by their grief that they need guidance and direction from someone outside their family circle. They need to be able to say, "This is what we want," and leave it to someone they trust to assure them that their wishes will be carried out. They need to be able to speak with that person, in small groups or privately, to address any tensions that may exist among them.

When my family planned for my mother's private service, we asked a close friend who is a college professor and experienced speaker to be in charge. He was also a dear friend of both my parents'. Although we had our ideas about what we wanted in the service, we left it to him to open our time together and lead us through the hour. Each of us had the opportunity to offer input, thus preventing any one of us (like me, the minister-daughter) from having a dominant role or excluding others who might have been reluctant to speak up in a family gathering.

Whoever conducts a memorial service is being trusted with the deepest and most precious of human feelings. Whoever accepts this task is holding a space for love and laughter, gratitude and sweet memory. This person is also holding a space for regret and guilt, anger and alienation. This is sacred space, where the human spirit is invited to touch and be touched by the holy—where there will be tears and thoughts that lie too deep for tears.

COMPOSING A SERVICE, BEGINNING TO END

Not long ago, I attended a memorial service that was planned and conducted by a friend of the bereaved family. It was in many ways a satisfying ceremony, providing space for people to share their memories of the person who had died. But the service leader conducted the service as if he were the master of ceremonies introducing one act after another. A memorial service is less like a variety show and more like a musical composition or a woven fabric. Each part, from beginning to end, is a part of the whole and contributes to the rhythm and mood of the entire service. Each part has a purpose, and participants need to know how they fit into the larger design, the fuller meaning. What I offer here is a description of the elements of a service and some suggestions for creating a rhythm that invites people to enter a space that is safe, healing, and transforming. I also share words I have used in services and explain why I use them, knowing that my approach may not suit everyone's needs. If you understand the purpose of each part, however, you can find or compose the words that will say it best. One of the resources I have found most useful is *Great Occasions: Readings for the Celebration of Birth, Coming-of-Age, Marriage, and Death,* edited by Carl Seaburg. This and other resources can be found in the list of reading recommendations at the end of the book.

Four elements are essential to nearly all ceremonies (with additional readings or music included as desired):

1. Opening remarks
   Setting the tone for the service
   Honoring the feelings of those who are gathered
   Naming the meaning of this gathering and including people who could not be present
   Speaking on behalf of family who may not be able to speak for themselves

2. Honoring and remembering the person who has died
   Composing a memorial portrait
   Personal remarks from family and friends

3. Invoking a spirit of gratitude, healing, and love (as in a litany or a prayer)

4. Offering words of blessing and inspiration for the living

Readings and Music

Readings and music nourish the soul, ground the spirit, and invite emotional release. They are not essential to the basic structure of a service, but they are often included for their power to offer spiritual nourishment and to touch universal chords of human feeling. Because of their power, they need to be carefully chosen, with an eye and an ear toward being as inclusive as possible of the various perspectives that people in attendance will have. In Western culture, it is likely that there will be Christians in attendance, even if the person who died was not Christian. If it does not offend the memory of that person, those people will derive comfort from hearing a familiar prayer or reading. Also, there have also been many instances in my experience when people who have abandoned their childhood tradition draw meaning from hearing the familiar words from that tradition. They are usually surprised by their own needs.

Readings

Any readings used in a memorial service should be selected intentionally and used sparingly. Most people do not come to a funeral to hear a sermon or philosophize about death. They come in the presence of death to grieve and reflect on what is meaningful in life; they come to be comforted and uplifted in their time of loss. Readings—a short poem, a scriptural selection—should be brief and should be chosen to serve a very specific purpose at a particular time in the service:

- At the start of the service, to define sacred space and invoke a holy presence for the time together
- As part of a eulogy or personal remarks, to invoke the person's presence—especially if the selection was written by the person, especially meaningful to the person, or particularly reflective of the person's life
- Before a selection of music, to comfort or offer reflection
- To lead into a time of meditation or prayer
- At the close of the service, to uplift and offer peace, hope, and promise

Music

Music is the language of the soul—a powerful source of healing. Its selection will be dictated by individual tastes and by the tone or style the family wants for the service. Like readings, however, music should be selected with the occasion and its other elements in mind. Unless you are holding a memorial concert, the music does not take center stage, it serves a purpose at a particular time.

For example, before the opening remarks, as people gather, music can invite people into the presence of the person who has died and make space for the emotions they bring. This is not the time to play "When the Saints Come Marching in." Neither do you need to play a dirge. The music should reflect the mood and the setting.

Use music once or at most twice during the service, as relevant. It may be introduced as something requested by or composed for the deceased. It may just be a quiet reflective piece following a prayer or reading. If music is likely to evoke powerful emotions, it should be used *only* at a time such as this. In the midst of the service is when people feel most safe; this is when tears can flow without needing to be stifled back. But that is precisely why it is not a good idea to place a powerful piece of music just before a close friend or family member is scheduled to speak.

After the closing words, a more upbeat or less emotionally charged selection may be appropriate. If the bereaved widow has to greet friends at an after-service reception, however, this is probably not the time to play the special song from her wedding.

Setting the Tone

Opening remarks set the tone and create space for what people are feeling. When I was a ministerial student, I attended a service being conducted by a prominent minister in Boston. During the first five minutes, he read several selections of poetry. I became restless. Why, I asked myself, doesn't he say something about why we are here? Why hasn't he mentioned the name of the person who died?

This was not the last time I asked these questions.

When you enter a space to honor someone who has died, you don't want to wait long before hearing what it is that has brought you there. And you want to hear a name—"dearly departed one" or "the deceased" just doesn't cut it. But just as you don't want five minutes of poetry about the meaning of death, you don't want to feel that someone is calling you into a meeting of the city council. The words that open a service define the space as holy and the time as sacred. This is particularly important when the space itself is not a traditional religious setting. The opening words invoke a spirit of love and healing to prevail. They may be offered in an informal setting but should never be offered casually. The first words spoken set the tone for the entire service.

What tone or style will be in keeping with the spirit of the person who is being remembered? Should it be dignified, warm, creative, pious, earthy, sophisticated, homespun? Whatever it is, it will come across as much in the presence of the person speaking and in the preparation of the meeting space as in the words spoken.

I usually begin a service with a greeting addressed to the people who have gathered. If I want a touch of formality, I use the whole name of the person who died. If I want a less formal, more intimate feeling, I use the first name only. Sometimes, when a more traditional beginning feels appropriate, I begin with selected lines from the third chapter of Ecclesiastes before offering a greeting. I do this because the words are familiar to most people and invite us to engage in a rite of passage that has brought human beings together since ancient times:

> For everything there is a season, and a time for every matter
> under heaven:
> A time to be born, and a time to die;
> A time to plant, and a time to pluck up what is planted; . . .
> A time to break down, and a time to build up;
> A time to weep, and a time to laugh;
> A time to mourn and a time to dance; . . .

For everything there is a season, and a time for every matter
under heaven.

Sometimes a simple greeting feels more like the place to begin:

Good afternoon, friends. I welcome you into this space, which is made
sacred in this season of loss with the spirit of love and friendship you bring
as you gather to remember _____. You come together as family, friends,
neighbors *(colleagues, classmates, coworkers, health professionals, hospice volunteers, and so on)*—cocreators of a community that includes those present but
also family and friends who could not be here today. We think particularly
of _____ *(names of any who are particularly missed)*. We come together that
we may honor _____ in our hearts and hold her/him dear in our memory.

Often there is something in the opening words that invites the spirit of
the person who has died into the space. For example, a family had prepared a
slide show for the service of a man whose idea of heaven was any place where
there was music. After the initial greeting, I said:

We have been called into this gathering with the chords of the organ. Music,
pictures, stories, and poems; tears, laughter, songs, and silence—each of these
shall offer us the medium for memory as we make _____ present with us.

In a service that was held outdoors, nature helped create a tone for the
opening:

In this lovely oak-sheltered setting, we come together as the family and friends
of _____. With grief and gratitude, we come to celebrate his life, to mourn
his death, to say good-bye. The family has chosen this setting, where we may
feel the freshness of the air and breathe the sweet fecund smell of earth. Here
we open ourselves to the spirit of life that flows through us all and repeats its

rhythms of death and birth, loss and renewal. They have chosen nature's sanctuary, that we may celebrate here the beauty and clarity of _____'s spirit.

And these words introduced a service that was held in the home of a man who had built his house:

On behalf of _____ *(his wife)* and her children, I welcome you here for this tribute to _____. As we gather here in this lovely room, we are welcomed not only by _____'s family but by _____ himself, for his presence is in every timber and beam of this home that he designed. This is space which has been made sacred with love and care and which we further consecrate with love and friendship.

Any service that is held in a home or yard opens in a setting where a person's presence is evoked in a variety of ways, and reminders of that presence can be named—creative decorating, a love for gardening or nature, a treasured sitting place, the environment of hospitality. As the space is prepared, there is an opportunity to consider and plan for what might be said to name briefly what it means to be in that place for this memorial visit.

The opening remarks should then incorporate information from the family interviews into a general statement of why everyone has come together: We have gathered to mourn a death and celebrate a life. We have also gathered to say good-bye. The general format is often something like this:

In this time we share today, we come to remember _____ and celebrate her life. We come also to mourn and say good-bye.

We come first to remember _____—to remember her as she was long ago and as she was just a few days *(weeks, months)* ago; to remember her in her times of strength and in her times of need; to remember her in her moments of joy or pleasure and in her moments of sadness; to remember her as she was—no more, no less.

In our remembering, we celebrate not only who she was but also what her life has meant and will always mean.

We come also to mourn—to mourn in the silent empty spaces once filled with her smiles, her companionship, her conversation; *(personalized remarks might refer to the sound of a person's laughter, the smell of good food cooking, a familiar phrase, and so on);* and to mourn the loss of her physical presence, the loss of love growing into tomorrow; . . .

Cite whatever losses seem appropriate. For a woman whose grandchildren were very young, for example, you might add, "to mourn for the opportunities her young grandchildren will not have to get to know her and for the opportunities she will not have to be with her children and grandchildren when they mark the passages of their lives." If there is a wedding, anniversary, birth, holiday, or other significant event coming up soon, this is the time to acknowledge the loss of being able to share it with this person.

Yes, we come to mourn—for the times that were and the times that were not; for the times that were and can no longer be; for the times that were not or cannot be.

Here one might name any particular losses that are not too private for the setting. Often people feel regret or sadness, not just because they will no longer enjoy the presence of a person who has died, but also because their time together was incomplete, their relationship conflicted or distant. The door has closed on the possibilities for reconciliation. A memorial service is not the time to announce these tensions or losses, but it is a time when they can be acknowledged without specific reference. If, for example, a young person dies and his father has not seen him for five years, that father bears the loss unlike any other mourner. It may be enough to say something general, speaking for those who have not had the opportunity to express their love or grow in relationship.

Sometimes the circumstances of death need to be named, particularly if death was sudden and unexpected or untimely. The following words were offered at the memorial for a man who died suddenly of a heart attack:

> _____'s quick and peaceful death was a gift for one who devoted so much of his life to helping others face death with dignity. Yes, it was as he would have wished it, but that did not offer time for good-byes, and some of you come with feelings of incompleteness or with thoughts of what you may not have said or done. Some of you come with poignant memories of the last time you were with him. May there be moments today that provide you the opportunity to offer your unspoken thoughts or prayers into this gathering of common memory and love.

When death is violent or untimely, chosen or mysterious, something needs to be said early in the service. (Some of these particular circumstances are discussed in greater depth in Chapter Six.)

After having named the losses and thus created space for mourning, the service leader can offer a statement that declares the primary purpose of the gathering. This too can be personalized, as in the following example:

> Most of all, we come today to invite _____'s presence with us and celebrate his life. Each of you comes with your own memories of _____, for he was not the same person to any two people here. Nor was he the same throughout his years with you, for he grew and changed as we all do. Today, as we celebrate his life and make him present with us, we bring images of a man who has touched our lives—images of his face, his laughter, his humor; images of

him in conversation, playing the piano, dancing, walking in the woods, or tinkering with an old car. These we bring into our common gathering, that the pain of losing him may be eased with the balm of love and memory. With tearful gratitude we come to honor and remember _____ today, that we may grow through an ending and, with memories gathered for the journey, gain strength for moving through the days and weeks ahead without him.

The Heart of the Service: A Life Remembered

When my mother died, we remembered her in an informal gathering where everyone was invited to share memories. When my father died, there were designated speakers. At my mother's service, I spoke; at my father's, I did not. There are no formulas for deciding who will speak and for how long.

It is entirely appropriate for the service leader to offer brief remarks before others speak. I will explain this in more depth in Chapter Five, which describes the process for creating a soul sketch or memorial portrait. The primary reason for this is to include the various perspectives that are represented in a family or a larger gathering. A husband, a child, a friend, a business partner—each of these had a different experience. One child may have been close to a parent; another not.

The soul sketch is brief and, like a pencil sketch, offers a glimpse into the complexities of a life lived in relationship (with self, with others, with the holy mysteries of life). It is then filled in by those who make personal remarks and give shading and definition to the sketch. It is not an essential part of the service, but it provides an inclusive introduction. It sets the stage for others who speak. In cases where families are alienated, perhaps not even on speaking terms, it is the only place where conflicting perspectives can be held up without being in conflict.

The real heart of the service is the words spoken by family and friends. During my sessions with family members, we talk about the options. One factor to consider is time. A memorial service is emotionally intense. Except in communities where people are accustomed to being in services longer, a service should not extend more than about an hour or so. If children are present (and they usually are), they will get restless and come to associate being in a memorial service with the feeling of wanting it to be over. Many adults will be just as restless, though they will not let it show.

If you want to keep a service within a particular time frame and are concerned about speakers taking too much time, you should give each speaker clear boundaries, perhaps inviting them to speak for less time than you actually expect them to use. For example, if you want someone to speak for five minutes, ask the person to speak for three.

It is more difficult to put limits on the time that family members use for their remarks. Only rarely will a family member use a public service in a way that is self-serving or insensitive. Most of the time, people are aware of the benefits of brevity. Their tributes are loving, poignant offerings from the heart, and listeners are always touched by what they say. Even when I have been well acquainted with the person we are honoring, I always feel his or her presence in the stories told by family and friends, and I always leave feeling that I have gotten better acquainted. Often I marvel at how many dimensions of a person are revealed in a memorial.

Whether the tributes are planned or spontaneous is up to those making the decisions. It will depend in part on their tolerance for the unpredictable and their willingness to have less control over who speaks. If spontaneous remarks are invited in addition to or instead of those planned, the time allotted for this part should be taken into account. In many services, after family and a few designated others speak, I make the following invitation to those gathered:

> During the next few minutes *(you can be specific about how many minutes if you wish)*, I invite some of you to share something of what it has meant to you to experience _____'s companionship, presence, wisdom, humor, or encouragement in your own lives *(this sentence can be personalized or made more general)*. You may wish to share a memory or say something about how your life has been enriched by _____. In this way, those of you who have known him/her make _____ present among us.
>
> Please speak briefly so that there will be time for several people to speak. Please stand and say who you are, and speak loudly enough for all to hear. *(If there is a microphone, you can adjust the instructions accordingly.)* If there are silent spaces between speakers, or if no one chooses to speak, you can use this time to nourish a silent memory or offer a prayer of gratitude.

It is important here to let people know what to expect and to invite their comfort with silence. Although people generally respect the request for brevity, there may be one or two who do not. For this reason, the service leader might stand during this time if it is a large gathering, offering a sense that someone is there to gently rein in the runaway speaker. This can be done with an affirming word of appreciation for their remarks or by saying something like, "You have more wonderful memories to share than we have time to hear today. I hope you will be able to find expression for them in conversation after the service."

After people have been given sufficient time to share their remarks, which ordinarily evoke both tears and laughter, the following words close this section:

> With tears and laughter, we dip into the deep well of love and memory. May these memories and those unspoken nourish you and keep _____ with you.

If there is a musical selection during the service, it may fit in well after this time of sharing.

For those who have less tolerance for the unpredictable but wish to invite people to share their memories, there is an alternative that was created by Betsy, who was dying following a long ordeal with cancer. It was the custom in her religious community for anyone who wanted to "share something" with the congregation to come forward following the eulogy. Sometimes the services could get quite long as a steady stream of friends came forward to offer their memories and express their loss. For the sake of her elderly frail mother, Betsy did not want her own memorial service to last a long time. Her minister arranged for each person who entered the sanctuary to receive a piece of lovely stationary and a pen.

During the service, the people in attendance were asked to write down a memory of Betsy or a few words of comfort for her family. At the conclusion of the service, they were invited to come forward and place their piece of stationary in a special box on an altar at the foot of the chancel. After the service, Betsy's mother and daughter could read the memories in private. Another family also used this ritual and chose to place the memories in a scrapbook that could later be shared with others.

Responsive Reading

A responsive reading invites participation. Unless a family has indicated an objection (which rarely occurs, even when they have no religious inclinations), I include my adaptation of a Jewish litany of memory (responsive reading) in every service and follow this with a prayer. Occasionally, the prayer is presented as a meditation. If you are not comfortable with traditional notions of prayer, there are suggestions in Chapter Three for how to invite holy space in alternative ways.

The reading, adapted from a modern Jewish liturgy by Roland B. Gittelsohn, has universal appeal.[1] In my introductory words, I provide a space for people to remember others as well as the person memorialized in the service. One grief stirs another, and many who gather are reminded of their own losses. This ritual brings us into that holy intimacy where we connect with one another on a spiritual level regardless of our religious beliefs. We move from our specific loss to recognition of our place in the cosmic rhythms of our universe. I have modified the litany, which is written as a responsive reading, so that there is no need for people present to have printed material. I begin with instructions for how we will do it:

I invite you to join in a litany of memory for _____, for _____ (*if there are other members of the deceased's family or community who are particularly missed, I name these persons along with the one we are memorializing*), and for others whom you hold dear in your memory. Please respond to each line that I read with the words, "We remember you."

In the rising of the sun and in its going down . . .
In the blowing of the wind and in the chill of winter . . .
In the opening of buds and in the rebirth of spring . . .
In the blueness of the sky and in the warmth of summer . . .
In the rustling of leaves and in the beauty of autumn . . .
In the beginning of the year and when it ends . . .
When we are weary and in need of strength . . .
When we are lost and sick at heart . . .
When we have joys we yearn to share . . .

Yes, we remember you. So long as we live, _____ too shall live, for she/he is a part of all who have known her/him.

In some gatherings and on other memorial occasions, families have used this litany, then followed the list with their own phrases: When I see a sun-flower . . . , ride a bicycle . . . , read a poem . . . ," and so on. This is a powerful way for people to participate, particularly if they shy away from public speaking. To introduce this variation, before the line, "Yes, we remember you," say,

And there may be other times that invoke _____'s memory in particular. I invite you now to add to this litany a phrase that comes to your mind, and we will all respond again to each phrase with the words, "We remember you."

Spoken Prayer

A spoken prayer touches the soul of community. When I plan services with families who are not comfortable with prayer, I tell them that I want to provide a time during the service for all of us to feel part of a community of caring. I also tell them that I want to use this time for an expression of gratitude. The prayer is offered into shared space, where its common expression provides a sacred dimension to the invocation to a spirit of healing, forgiveness, and renewal. What I say in the prayer will be personalized for the family and the person remembered, but it will usually include some of the following expressions:

Let us pause in the spirit of prayer:
Spirit of life and mystery, we pause now to be still, to breathe in each moment of life with a sense of gratitude for its gifts of beauty, love, and grace. We pause to affirm the cycles of life and of death, for we know that we are all part of an endless and mysterious cycle of existence.

But there is deep pain and loss in these days, and so we pause before the mystery of life and death to pray. We name in our hearts all who grieve this loss, particularly *(names discussed with the family and included with their advance knowledge)*. May they be lifted on wings of love and hope and receive a balm of healing. Where there lingers any misunderstanding, alienation, or regret, we ask for the healing of forgiveness; where there has been warmth and love, we evoke the healing power of gratitude.

We also give thanks for _____'s kind and generous spirit and for the legacy _____ leaves in this world. We give thanks for the light of love that persists through death and lives in human hearts.

All of this we offer as our common prayer. Amen.

The service closes, most often, with a poem or a benediction (or both). Several suitable readings, prayers, and blessings are presented in Resource Three.

CELEBRATING LIFE AND MOURNING DEATH

A friend told me recently that the trouble with a lot of memorial services these days is that they do not create space for the tears to flow. People want to celebrate a life but are afraid to mourn a death. An effective memorial service will do both. Like a great musical composition or dramatic production, it will follow a pattern or rhythm that allows participants to move gradually into emotional depths where they may release the passions and burdens of their grieving hearts. Then the flow brings them back into a space where, with memories gathered for the journey, they affirm hope and promise for the days ahead. The arrangement of all elements should keep this sense of aesthetic flow in mind.

CHAPTER THREE

Inviting Holy Space

Prayers and Meditations,
Candles and Poetry

PLEASE DON'T PRAY OVER ME," MY AUNT SAID WHEN I WENT TO VISIT HER A few weeks before her death. I am not sure what it was she did not want, but I suspect she imagined I would talk to God on her behalf. I remember having a similar aversion to prayer when a minister came to visit me once in a hospital. He meant well, but his patriarchal language and theology were not a comfort to me.

If you are comfortable with prayer and prayer is a regular part of your spiritual life, this chapter will affirm some of the reasons it is important to you. The richer your own spiritual life is, the more it will serve you in times of loss and grief.

If, however, you are like my aunt, and perhaps even consider your life spiritually full, this chapter will challenge you to consider what prayer does for the spirit and introduce you to alternatives that may help you and others through times of loss and grief.

As a Unitarian Universalist minister, I am often in the position of offering a "prayer" as part of a community gathering. The challenge is always to be inclusive of a variety of perspectives, including people who have no belief in a deity. So instead of saying, "Let us pray," I will suggest we join in a *spirit* of prayer or meditation. On one occasion, a member of my congregation noted that people in other religions use prayer as a way to connect with the infinite, the core, the fundamental meaning of things. Although she did not pray, she wanted to make a prayerful connection. She then posed the question, "If you don't pray, what do you do?"

Religious liberals have been described as praying "to whom it may concern." In truth, many spiritually oriented people do not pray—at least not in a traditional way. It is a matter of personal preference how a prayer is addressed (if indeed it is addressed at all): Father; Mother; Allah; Jesus; God; Goddess; the Tao that has no name; the Light; the Dark; the Blessed; the Mysterious; Spirit of Life; Spirit of Holiness; Spirit of Love, Peace, and Hope; Nameless One; Eternal One; Beloved Presence; Creator of the Universe; and so on. If you address a divine presence (or absence), it may be with many names or with no name; it may be the Spirit among us and within us as much as the Spirit beyond our knowing.

If you are skeptical about whether or not God has ears, it does not mean that you do not want to connect with a deeper source of wisdom, goodness, and hope. I know many hard-core atheists who feel a deep and spiritual connection with the cosmic energy that sustains creation.

Even the most skeptical agnostics still have the human needs to do what others do with prayer—to offer gratitude, to praise beauty, to confess personal failures, to dedicate their lives to a path of goodness, to cry out in despair, or to call on the powers of healing or strength.

So if you don't pray, what do you do? You create inner space, which is where you become more comfortable with yourself in all space.

And how do you do it? Many ways. What makes the difference is not what you do but the consciousness in your heart and mind as you do it.

For some people, meditation is an effective way to create inner space. Depending on what fits your personal style, this might be Zen meditation or Transcendental Meditation or something you have devised. It might be a walking or breathing meditation, as taught by Thich Nat Hanh. You might apply a Hindu's devotion to cutting vegetables or a Native American's reverence to planting a garden or a Sufi's universal love to dancing. Perhaps you take a daily walk on the beach or in the woods—a walk in beauty and gratitude and reverence.

I have discovered that I respond to what Matthew Fox calls "extrovert meditation" or "art as meditation."[1] If I play the drum or walk or swim with a consciousness of immersing in the rhythms of life, it creates inner space. The same is true if I put on a tape of a chant and light a candle, then just sit and let the chant sing through my body.

If you set aside even a few minutes a day for creating inner space, you invite a spirit of peace and healing to abide in the soul and offer nourishment for even the tiny losses that occur in your daily life: your favorite vase is broken; you need new glasses; your computer ate your homework. It is not easy, however, to maintain a schedule in which inner-space time is created, and a bit of extra discipline may be required to be sure the spirit is not neglected.

A few years ago, while my husband and I had our grandchildren living with us for three months, some of my routines for creating inner space were interrupted. Instead of meditating in the early morning hours, I was packing lunch and making breakfast and talking with children. I had to adjust. I became very sympathetic with parents of young children. I often went through days feeling more in touch with outer space than with inner space. I took more baths, using the time in the bathtub to create inner space.

Knowing that I had to have some inner-space time, I carved out about fifteen minutes in the evening to sit outside and watch the sun set. Jennafer, my seven-year-old granddaughter, caught on and wanted to join me. I was annoyed at first, and then I explained to her why I wanted that quiet time with the sky. I told her what kind of time and space this was before she came into it, and she understood. So we cuddled under a blanket as the sky darkened and watched the stars come out. As the first star appeared, we shared that moment of wonder, saying, "Star light, star bright, first star I see tonight. I wish I may, I wish I might, have the wish I wish tonight." In the context of creating inner space, it was a form of prayer.

If we do no more than pause for two minutes of silence or light a candle or sound a bell and invite focus, we create inner space.

In that space, we recognize that the divine spirit dwells within us and among us.

When death intrudes on our lives and disrupts or destroys structures of relationship that give us meaning, we are more aware of this inner space and our need to cultivate it. I am not saying anything new here, of course—just offering a reminder to those whose inner space has been invaded and taken over by outer space.

Yes, you may know this, but what do most people do when they have experienced a loss? They try to keep themselves busy. They seek distraction. It is a coping mechanism. It is also a human impulse to avoid pain.

Cultivating inner space is not a coping mechanism; it is a spiritual habit. It is more likely to take you into the pain than out of it; through the pain rather than above it; beyond the pain rather than around it. Even if all you can do is carve out ten minutes for a regular bathtub meditation or a few moments at dusk to wish on a star, your awareness of inner space will be there to help you through the heart-wrenching and life-shattering times of grief that will surely come your way.

CREATING A CARING SPACE

One summer when I was visiting in North Carolina from California, my granddaughter Jennafer was attending day care at the Baptist Church. I would frequently pick her up there in the afternoons. In the lobby, I saw a long list of names on a bulletin board. At first I thought they were probably people who gave to a building fund. Then I saw the heading over the names. It read, "Intercessory Prayers." Intercessory prayers are those offered on behalf of others. I read the names then with a prayerful attitude, knowing that each was in need of strength or healing for reasons I did not know.

Several years ago, before Eastern Airlines got gobbled up, the company was in a state of some distress. As I checked in for a flight, I asked the woman at the counter how she was doing. The tears began to flow, and she told me she was looking for another job. I went to the boarding area to wait for my flight and was surprised when she came over to me. Apparently she had seen "Reverend" next to my name. She told me that she had changed my seat to first class. Then she said, "Please pray for me, Reverend."

Prayer creates a caring space.

I told the young woman I would pray for her, and I did.

I like the way the Quakers express it. "I hold you in the Light," they say. That's a beautiful concept.

I do not always pray for people in a traditional way, but I keep a written list of the names of those I want to hold in the Light. It goes on a tag that I stick to my desktop, where I will see it several times a day. As I say people's names, I hold them in the Light. This is more than thinking of them or caring for them or wishing them health. I call on a transcendent and mysterious power that I cannot name.

Scientific studies have been conducted to determine the power of prayer to heal people with illness. Some of these studies have demonstrated that even when people were not aware that others were praying for them, they have shown greater improvement than those in control groups.[2]

This research suggests that somewhere in the mysteries of our universe, there might be a power—a healing power—available to us. It suggests that if all who gather in a community of caring offer a prayer or hold one another in the Light, it makes a difference.

When we gather in community and hold someone in the Light, we invite a healing power. We invite the power of love and grace. We invite the power of forgiveness and hope and reconciliation. We invite the power of inner strength and peace.

Whether or not you pray, it is important to hold those who suffer or grieve in the Light and to say out loud, in another's presence, that you are doing this. Light a candle and say a name—that is enough. Or join in a circle, inviting images of love and gratitude into the circle. If you are comfortable using that circle in a physical way to embrace a person in pain or grief, do it. If not, try doing it in words. I have participated in many communities where healing circles were offered. On a few occasions, feeling the need for the physical feeling of being held in the Light, I entered the circle and felt the loving energy that gathered in the center where I was held and held up. It works. Whether prayers are spoken, chanted, or offered in a silent touch, this circle of caring works. There is a remarkable power in the sense of spiritual connection with others, known and unknown.

My colleague Rob Eller-Isaacs says, "I don't really know if prayer makes things happen. But I have no doubt, prayer makes love flow."

CREATING A RECEPTIVE SPACE

I like the Zen story about a learned university professor of Asian studies who visited a master at a temple in Japan. The master received the professor in his private room, and an attendant served tea. As soon as he had seated himself, the professor began talking on and on about Zen philosophy. The master said nothing as he poured the tea into his guest's cup. The professor hardly noticed and kept talking and talking—he felt, in fact, wonderfully inspired.

Suddenly he realized that the Zen master was still pouring tea even though the cup had long since overflowed, and the tea had spilled out onto the tatami mat. And still the master continued pouring.

"Stop, stop, what are you doing?" cried the professor. The master looked up. "Just as the cup cannot hold anymore tea when it is already filled," he said, "how can I give you anything when your mind is already filled?"[3]

Prayer creates a receptive space. We can pray without words. If we are good at it, we can pray without thoughts. Most of us aren't so good at it. We are too full of our worries or plans or daily concerns. Our task is to empty ourselves so that we can receive the gifts and challenges of a greater self. I do not mean to imply that this is an easy task. You can speak with people who have cloistered themselves in religious communities for many years, and they will tell you that they have not mastered the practice of emptying, even through hours of meditation.

INVITING A HOLY PRESENCE

In a *Peanuts* comic strip by cartoonist Charles Schulz, Charlie Brown says to Lucy, "May I ask you a personal question, Lucy?"

"Why, of course," she answers. Then Charlie Brown says, "I don't want to upset you." Lucy replies, "Don't be silly Charlie Brown. . . . Nothing you ask could possibly upset me!" He then looks directly at her and says, "Do you pray before you go to bed or after you get up in the morning?" Lucy responds by opening her mouth wide and letting out a deep anguished cry.

Many people have some awkwardness around the notion of prayer. When I am in the company of people who think we ought to offer a blessing before a meal, for example, they will usually ask me to do it, rather than doing it themselves.

One of the primary reasons people pray is to connect with a holy presence and to feel its power in their lives. Such a power can be (and should be) frightening. Annie Dillard warns people who go to church to consider what power they "so blithely invoke." She writes, "The churches are children playing on the floor with their chemistry sets, mixing up a batch of TNT to kill a Sunday morning. It is madness to wear ladies' straw hats and velvet hats to church; we should all be wearing crash helmets. Ushers should issue life preservers and signal flares; they should lash us to our pews. For the sleeping god may wake someday and take offense or the waking god may draw us out to where we can never return."[4]

Inviting the Holy into our midst and into our lives is not always an invitation to peace and serenity, for we are inviting a power that is beyond our own. We seek to be forgiven for those times we haven't measured up, and we want inspiration and power for becoming our better selves. We call on a power of strength when we feel weak. We know our failings, our longings. Confronting the mystery of death, the horror of suffering, or the hollow emptiness of our loneliness, we are vulnerable.

What we discover is that in transition periods especially, we are vulnerable to joy as well as pain. When I recall some of the peak experiences of my life, I realize that many epiphanies have occurred when I was in transition or crisis. A door was opened to intimacy with others. After my father died, for example, my older brother and I became much closer. We talked about our lives, discussing— guess what?—our *feelings* about what it meant to grow up in our family. Because we were two adults "orphaned" together, we recognized that we shared some experiences with one another that no one else shared. Each of us realized that the other was our sole connection with childhood (our younger brother had died six months before our father). From that time on, we have related on a deeper level. This means we confront tensions with one another with more honesty. It means we enjoy being together. It means we love one another, not just because we are family, but because we are companions on life's brief journey.

Any experience of death and loss—even one intensified with years of resentment or alienation—summons us into a more intimate space with others— to be more honest with one another, to seize the day, settle our differences, open our souls, risk judgment. In short, we are invited to be fully human and to feel the grace of the Spirit at work in our lives.

Thus, too, we are more intimate with the spirit of life—no armor, no protective shell. Our calendar is cleared for the agenda of being human, of connecting with the Spirit and with others as we seldom do when our days are filled with errands and appointments. At no other time are we more open to the grace and promise of the Spirit than when we allow our naked souls to touch and be touched by the Holy.

No wonder Lucy let out a cry of anguish. What could be more personal, more fragile, or more vulnerable than the part of each of us that yearns to connect with something holy and eternal and at the same time fearfully recoils from being deeply moved? We live in these aging, decaying bodies and are reminded daily that they will eventually fail us. Still, we long to connect with the very source of goodness and love that prevails through all and will not fail.

When we pray, then, or do whatever it is we do instead of prayer, we invite something of the timeless into this moment, something of eternity into the now. We celebrate beauty and love and hope. We acknowledge and confront our fear and our weakness and our imperfection before the mysteries of the universe.

Victor Hugo once wrote, "Certain thoughts are prayers. There are moments when, whatever the attitude of the body, the soul is on its knees."

Even if we don't pray, certain thoughts are prayerful. With them, we create a space where the soul is on its knees, inviting a holy presence to bless us, to bless those we love, and to bless the world.

A CIRCLE OF LOVE

When I have the opportunity to be with a family when someone is near death, I usually invite them into a bond of common prayer. Sometimes I am the only one who says anything. Sometimes others speak too. We are all held in the Light in a moment of profound grief, love, and mystery.

Many people who are not comfortable with prayer, however, want to be able to participate in a prayerful way. Inspired by Stephen Levine's use of meditation, I have created a meditation that offers opportunities for family members to "pray" in ways that are less threatening for them. I first used it for the family of Bill Cosdon. Bill's wife, Judy, was humanistic in her approach to religion; in contrast, one of his daughters was a Christian. I wanted each of them to have space for expression.

For years, Bill had carried on a valiant battle with cancer, drawing on his own spiritual resources to triumph through many crises. He was losing the last round, and his spirit was directed toward living well through his dying. As he slipped into a semiconscious state, unable to speak but showing signs of being partially aware of what occurred near him, the family gathered from distant places, and Judy asked me to be with them. After I met with them for a few minutes to tell them what I wanted to do, we all gathered around Bill's bed. I told him we were there to hold him in a circle of love and light, and we each gently put our hands on him. In some traditions, this is called "the laying on of hands." Having experienced the power that is transmitted through such a ritual when I was ordained, I can testify that the touch of those who gather in this fashion to offer their love and create a circle of blessing transmits a remarkable spiritual power.

Members of the family were then invited to express their feelings to Bill. Each of them did this, tears spilling generously as they spoke from their hearts. They told him that they were there with him and that they would be OK when he was gone. Then I told Bill that we wanted to offer a meditation together. I had assigned the parts to those who gathered so that each person could speak separately.

The meditation was a blessing, a prayer of release, a message of peace. In it, the family became agents of a Spirit that is eternal, holy, and loving:

> I am the wind, breathing in you and for you, blowing gently
>   over you, caressing you.
> I am the earth, holding you. Give me the weight of your body
>   and relax into my arms.
> I am the sun, warming you, melting away the cares of this world.
> I am the mountain, always here for you, always here for you,
>   always here for you.
> I am a river, flowing through you—through your head, your
>   neck, your shoulders, your arms, your body, your legs, your
>   feet. I give you peace.
> I am the ocean, rising and falling, giving you deep beauty and rest.
> I am the sky, open space never-ending, open space, vast and
>   edgeless space, where you may float forever and ever.
> I am the Light, the Light of eternal spirit. I am all around you.
>   I am in this world and in all worlds, for I am the Light of all
>   being.
> (all together): I am peace, I am spirit, I am love, I am life growing
>   into new life.

Shortly after this ritual, Bill died. There is no way to know what he may have felt or heard, but this ritual was a powerful passage for Bill and his family. I have offered this meditation to many families since, and they have experienced a similar sense of having participated in a loving passage. In some cases, the meditation was offered shortly after death, serving to assist those gathered in their process of closure and letting go. In one case, a family could not handle doing the ritual in the presence of the person who was dying. Conscious of his nearness to death as he struggled to breathe in his hospital bed, we gathered in the hospital chapel and spoke the lines of the meditation for him.

I have not always been able to be present with family and friends for this circle, so I have given them copies of the meditation to read, with instructions for the circle and the laying on of hands. After witnessing what one family did with this ritual, hospice volunteers, touched by the power of this simple gathering, requested copies to use with their patients. They had found themselves in the position of advising families that patients sometimes need to be given "permission" to die; this ritual, however, offered families a spiritual context for this difficult offering of release.

LIGHTING CANDLES OF HOPE, LOVE, LIGHT, AND PEACE

I am not Catholic, but I love cathedrals and seldom enter one without being drawn to the rows and rows of candles that represent a multitude of sorrows, joys, and prayers. Depending on what prayers lay dormant in my own soul, I always light a candle or two.

There is something universally prayerful about lighting a candle. And there are more ways to use candles for remembering than I could name here. It has been my experience that most people instinctively know what they want to say with the growing light, and the gesture itself is its own voice of hope.

Maureen Killoran, the minister of the church I now attend, offers her opening remarks for memorial services, then lights a single white taper. Using a quotation from J. Donald Johnston, she says, "In the presence of Life, we say *no* to Death. In the presence of Death, we say *yes* to Life."[5]

The single candle flickers throughout the service. At the end, just before her closing words, she takes the candle from its holder and says, "_____'s body is no longer with us, but his/her spirit lives on." She then blows out the flame and gives the candle to the next of kin. The moment when the candle is extinguished and handed to this person is particularly powerful. The service ends with a sense of the light that family and friends carry with them as they leave.

Another minister reports that at some services there will be a copper tray with sand in it. People are invited to come forward and "speak briefly" or in silence, light a candle in honor of the one who has died, and place it upright in the sand. As the glow increases with the addition of candles, it becomes very apparent that the life of the person continues in the lives of others.

Such a ceremony could also be planned for a small family gathering—a private opportunity to experience the persistence of light through a time of sharing memories.

Candles can also invite the darkness, offering a comfortable and less fearful way to spend time in it. Although we are accustomed to think of a candle as symbolic of our human resistance to death, there are also times when it becomes a decoration in the mystery of a welcome dark. It says yes to death, and those who carry the light enter the dark with peace and hope.

A BODY PRAYER

Some people relate to expressing prayer through their bodies, through dance or walking meditation, yoga, and so on. There is a body prayer that I have incorporated into my spiritual practice that can be very nourishing to even the most physically inhibited individuals. It is also meaningful as a shared experience with a group of people. If you wish for the prayer to give you healing energy through times of pain and grief, it may be useful to name what you need from it at the beginning. Here are the basic motions, all of which should be done slowly and with a feel for the rhythm of each gesture:

1. Begin by standing erect with your palms together in front of your chest or face.

2. Bow reverently, honoring the Holy as you understand it.

3. As you return to an erect position, keep your hands together, but bring them up in front of your face, raise them over your head, and then separate them and reach up as if to open your whole self to receiving the gifts of the Holy into your being.

4. Bring your arms back down slowly, and cross them onto your chest one over the other, in a motion that gathers the spiritual gifts or healing energy you have received and brings it into your being.

5. Opening your arms and reaching out before you with your palms open, feel yourself giving a divine or healing energy back into the world, sharing it with others.

6. Bring your palms back together in front of your chest or face.

7. After your palms are back together, clap once, in a gesture of keeping awake and receptive to the gifts of the Holy that are there for you in the moment.

8. With your palms together as in the beginning, bow again.

9. Repeat as many times as you wish, ending with a bow.

POETRY: MORE LANGUAGE OF THE SOUL

In Chapter Two, I warned against overloading a memorial service with too many readings. The impact of one poem can be very powerful. It is often diluted by a second or a third poem. That said, I only want to say here that poetry can also be a form of prayer, for its imagery and music reach into the soul's depths and touch it in ways that go beyond any understanding of what the words may say or mean.

Some poetry does not play well, however, when read aloud. Poems need to be chosen not only for their appropriate placement in the rhythm of a service or ritual but also for their readability and clarity when spoken to a diverse group. Short is also better than long. I rarely use a poem that is longer than sixteen lines.

Do not be afraid to adapt a poem to the occasion and to say that you are doing so. I have told my husband that I want a poem by William Blake read at my memorial, but with all the male pronouns changed to female:

> She who binds herself to a joy
> Doth the winged life destroy;
> But she who kisses the joy as it flies
> Lives in eternity's sunrise.[6]

A SEA OF PRAYER

Prayers are offered in so many ways. As the Reverend Carolyn Colbert puts it, we live in "a sea of prayer":

> I have this notion that we live in a sea of prayer. All over the world, in almost all traditions, prayer is being practiced. Practiced in a multitude of forms. Prayers are chanted, prayers are danced, prayers are spoken aloud and sounded in silence within. Prayers are written on paper and scattered like petals on the waters of the world. Some prayers are floated out on the breath; others are pounded out on the drumbeat of our hearts. Prayers are said and sung and danced morning noon and night. They are flung to the wind by flapping flags and spun into the air by turning wheels. Prayers are shouted from the tops of majestic mountains and whispered by children at bedtime in the close and holy darkness.

Amen. So be it. Blessed be.

CHAPTER FOUR

Decisions

Thinking When You Are
Least Able to Think

ALICE HAD PICKED UP THE CHILDREN AT SCHOOL AND STOPPED BY THE grocery store. The phone rang while she was unloading groceries. Bobby, twelve, had already taken off on his bike for the basketball court, and Shawna, six, was in her room playing with her Barbie dolls.

It was John, her husband's boss. Terry had had a heart attack and had been taken to the hospital. She needed to get there right away. She left the groceries on the counter as she gathered Shawna into the car. They went by the park to pick up Bobby.

When Alice arrived at the hospital emergency room, John and his wife, Diane, greeted her and introduced her to the hospital chaplain.

"Where is my husband?" Alice asked. "I want to see him."

"They're still working on him," said John, looking toward the chaplain. "Chaplain Sanders will keep us informed. She has opened a private room for us."

What they did not tell Alice or the children was that Terry had already died. Once they were in private quarters, the doctor entered. Without sitting down, he delivered the news. Alice, conscious of the children and unable to take it all in, picked up only snatches of his conversation. "We understand that your husband collapsed at work . . . ambulance . . . were able to restart his heart . . . another attack . . . could not maintain . . . I'm so sorry . . ."

Suddenly Alice, known for her ability to take charge of major fundraising events, organize a household, work part time, and serve dinner to thirty guests without a hitch, did not have any idea what to do.

After giving everyone time to take in the overwhelming news and cry the tears of initial devastation, the chaplain asked Alice if she would like to see Terry.

"Yes," she said, still numb with shock. "Can the children come?"

"They can if they want to, but I think you may need to spend some time with him first," Chaplain Sanders replied. Chaplain Sanders spoke with the children. "Bobby, Shawna, do you want to go see your dad? If you don't feel like you can, it's OK. Some grown-ups want to go and some just can't. He will look very quiet, almost like he is sleeping, but very still."

The children only knew they wanted to be with their mother. Alice said she felt it was important for the children to have an opportunity to say good-bye to their father.

"I will go see if the nurses are ready," said the chaplain, sensing that the family needed a little more time.

"We will need to know what funeral home you want to use," Chaplain Sanders told Alice later. "If you need time to discuss this with other family members, I can give you a number to call us later."

"I don't know. We never talked about . . . I need to talk to his mother and brothers."

Chaplain Sanders directed Alice to the phone and then left to check with the nurses about where the family could see Terry. Meanwhile, the nurse called Lifeshare (the organ donation organization). Terry was a potential candidate for donating corneas, whole eyes, and bone.

Within an hour after Terry's death, Alice, in shock and grief, and conscious of her two children, had to make no less than four important decisions:

Did she want to see Terry?

Did she want the children to see him?

Did she want to give consent to Lifeshare for organ donations?

Who would be called to come for Terry's body?

The doctor was certain that Terry had died of a massive heart attack and so did not see the need for an autopsy. This meant that the tube could be removed from Terry's mouth, making it easier for the family to see him, particularly the children. If the circumstances of death were questionable, a medical examiner could have requested an autopsy, and the tube would have had to remain.

Alice was fortunate to have a chaplain to assist her. Still, she was not in a state of mind to think quickly. How much better it would have been if she and Terry had given some thought to what they would do in the event of sudden death.

Alice was not a religious person, but she was grateful when the chaplain offered to help her and the children say good-bye to Terry. John and Diane went with them to a room in a corner of the Emergency Room area. The nurse had closed Terry's eyes, and his mouth was slightly open. Covered with a sheet and blanket, he looked peacefully still. Alice went right to him, hugged him, and kissed him. The children stood back. Chaplain Sanders said, "It's OK to touch him if you want." Bobby went closer and touched his father's arm; then

Shawna, holding her mother's hand, touched him also. The chaplain gave them time to be with him, and Alice spent some time in the room alone while John and Diane took the children to the snack bar. Alice also took time to speak with a representative from Lifeshare on the phone and fill out consent forms. It was very difficult for her to do this, but she liked thinking of ways that Terry's tragic death could help another person.

Terry's brother, the only other family member living in the vicinity, came by with his partner. Before they all left the hospital, the chaplain, sensitive to Alice's discomfort with religious rituals, invited them to create a circle of blessing to say good-bye to Terry together. Not knowing whether or not she would choose cremation, Alice was aware that this could be the last time they would have with him.

The chaplain invited everyone to gather around Terry's bed. Each person who wanted to do so spoke to him, declaring his or her love and receiving tissues and hugs from the others gathered. Then the chaplain invited everyone to repeat the following words after her together: "Terry (or Daddy), we love you. We will miss you so much. You will always be with us in our hearts. Bless you." (The chaplain had selected these words as appropriate and true after conversations with the family.) Each member of the group then offered a personal good-bye (a touch, a kiss) before leaving the room.

TO VIEW OR NOT TO VIEW?

In the months and years that followed Terry's death, Alice was grateful that she and her children had had this opportunity to say good-bye before his body was removed from the hospital. There was a brief window of time when he was still Terry, not a body for professionals to mine for organs, then cremate or preserve. Once that window closed, the opportunity was gone.

Yes, it was painful to see him. The tears flowed—the first sobs among many that were part of a healthy grieving process. Still stunned by the news of his death, their time with him helped them accept the reality of it. Alice decided that she wanted Terry's body cremated, but she also wanted other members of the family to have an opportunity to see him, so she arranged with the funeral home to keep his body available long enough to give them time. Terry's mother chose not to see him, saying that she wanted to remember him alive, not dead.

There are no set guidelines on this matter of whether or not to spend time with a person's body shortly after he or she has died. I have been with many families who, like Alice, have been grateful when they did. This has almost always been the case when death was sudden or the person died very young. Even after a person has been ill for a long time and death is a welcome release from suffering, I recommend that families take a few moments to offer parting words or prayers in an intentional way. Like any good leave-taking, this face-to-face good-bye can assist the process of grief. Those who are able to offer their parting words or gestures in these precious and poignant moments are taking advantage of an opportunity that will never come again.

Each person should be given the opportunity for private time; then all who are present before a body is removed (particularly if it is taken from their home) can gather in a simple circle and offer a joint farewell. At this time, particularly if this is their last contact, they may want to anoint the body and offer a final blessing. That blessing can be something as simple as the words the chaplain invited Alice's family to repeat. Or it might be a song or chant or perhaps familiar and comforting words from religious scripture. The words are less important than the power of gathering together in a loving way.

When a family has chosen to have a body embalmed or plans to keep the body somewhere "on ice" for a day or so, they also have the option of holding a more public viewing. This is each family's decision, influenced by past experience and the family's religious or cultural traditions. Although it is rarely practiced in my tradition, I have heard from many people that a viewing was particularly helpful after the death of a child.

Allison, for example, was eight years old when she died of a brain tumor. Her parents were not inclined to hold a viewing, but the social worker who had helped them through the child's illness persuaded them to do so. At the funeral home, a separate section of the room was designated for children, and in it there were several kinds of art and craft materials, from clay to crayons, from felt to felt-tipped pens. There had been a notice in the obituary informing people that there would be special children's activities at the viewing and that Allison's friends were encouraged to attend. Allison's teacher also called each family in her class with a personal invitation. When children arrived, they were invited to go to the children's corner where they could make something for Allison. Hospice social workers helped the children and encouraged them to view Allison, which most of them did. Some went alone; some went in small groups; some found a parent to accompany them. Some wept; some looked in silence; some whispered to one another. One or two actually touched Allison. For most of them, the viewing helped them reach a kind of closure and comfort with death. One five-year-old child viewed Allison, then said to his mother, "Gosh, Mom, she looked just like you said she would, but you didn't tell me her shoes would be so beautiful!"

Families confront a more difficult decision if someone has died in a violent manner and the person's body has been mutilated, perhaps even beyond recognition. Such was the case for Nicolas, whose nineteen-year-old son was bludgeoned to death by a desperate stranger, leaving his face and skull an unrecognizable chunk of bone and blood. When Nicolas went to the morgue, it was not to identify his son's body but to say good-bye. Warned by the staff that the youth was badly mutilated, Nicholas still chose to view his son.

I do not know why this was the man's choice. I can guess that whether or not he saw his son's body, he would be haunted by images of mutilation, real or imagined. I can also guess that he needed to see his son's body, in whatever condition, in order to accept the horror of his death.

I was deeply moved by another parent's need to touch what was left of her daughter's body after it had been so badly mangled in machinery that only a few parts had been salvaged. Her minister accompanied the mother to the funeral home, and they met with considerable resistance when they requested to see the daughter's body. The funeral director, visibly disturbed by the condition of this teenager's body himself, was horrified by the notion of a mother seeing her child's body in pieces. After the minister's insistence that the mother view at least a small, more presentable portion of the body, the funeral director finally agreed to allow one hand to appear outside the drape. The mother sat for almost two hours stroking that hand—looking at each finger, the creases of the palm, the remnants of iridescent pink nail polish that still sparkled from corners of her nails. The minister offered a brief blessing, and the mother kissed her daughter's hand in a gesture of final parting.

Years later, this mother expressed her gratitude to the minister, affirming what an important part of her grieving took place there.

TO CREMATE OR NOT TO CREMATE?

In 1998, my stepson Tom chose to end his life. He left instructions with his wife for the committal of his body. Cremate my body, he requested, and distribute the ashes on Moores Pond. After a memorial service at the funeral home chapel, family members went to the spot he had chosen. Tom's wife opened the box of ashes and hesitated a moment. It was obvious that she wanted to use her hands but was unsure whether or not others might be offended. "You can touch them," I said. I had already warned the family that the ashes may contain some large bone fragments. Each of us threw a handful or two of Tom's cremated remains in the water. Following this, we each took a flower from an arrangement we had brought down to the dock and threw it on the water. For a few moments, the powdery dust of Tom's ashes still on our hands, we watched as the red roses drifted slowly away from the dock.

The choice for cremation was Tom's choice, and we honored his request. More and more people choose cremation, perhaps because it gives them opportunities to place the ashes in a location that holds meaning for them. Some choose cremation because it is less expensive than interment or because they cannot gather the family for several months to hold a memorial. Most people who choose cremation, however, do so because this choice in some way reflects their values, their spiritual perspective, or their philosophy about life and death. I have heard critics of cremation say that it demonstrates a denial of the natural process of physical decay that comes with death—an avoidance of the pain of dealing with a dead body. Others support cremation as the option that least denies death, particularly because it does not preserve the body but rather surrenders the body with a realistic understanding that the true essence of the person who lived in that body is no longer there. Whether or not cremation or burial is a denial of death or an avoidance of the pain of grief is not a function of what choice is made but rather of what emotional processes drive that choice.

So I cannot advise people regarding their preference. I do recommend, however, giving some thought to the options that exist and taking some time to think about what each represents.

First, who makes the decision? My personal request is to be cremated and have my ashes distributed on the North Carolina property where we have planted or scattered the remains of my parents, my younger brother, my stepson Tom, and several dogs. But I cannot dictate to my husband what will feel right to him, and I do not want him to do anything that is not comfortable for him. So I have not asked him to sign any irrevocable promises to carry out my wishes. His instructions to me (or other survivors, if I die before he does) are different. He wants his body cremated and the ashes distributed in three different locations. Some of his remains he wants to have placed near mine (and those of my family) in North Carolina. He also wants a portion in his ancestral home in England and a portion in the cemetery where members of his family have been interred. Had he not shared this request with me, it would not have occurred to me to purchase a cemetery plot or to travel to England with a portion of his ashes.

Second, there are usually several family members who care about what happens, and any decision should involve them in conversation that allows them to express their issues or concerns. If my husband does not outlive all of us, I will honor his request after consulting with other members of the family.

Alice's decision with regard to Terry's body was unusual, but it was made after she consulted with his family. She had already called a funeral home that was recommended by friends and was fortunate to work with a funeral director who respected her financial restrictions and was sensitive to her needs. Terry's body was kept in a temperature-controlled locker and did not require embalming, and there was no disturbing evidence of organ donations that had been made to Lifeshare. The family members who wanted to see him were able to do so before the body was cremated.

Those who choose not to cremate do not have to choose to have the body embalmed. They should know in advance, however, that they will opt for a quick burial or will provide for a way to keep the body preserved. Immediate burial is the custom in most Jewish communities, where bodies are neither cremated nor embalmed and funerals are generally held shortly after a death.

DIRECT HANDS-ON INVOLVEMENT

What Alice did not have the opportunity to consider is an option that most people are not even aware they have. I admit that I did not know of this option until I read Natalie Goldberg's book, *Long Quiet Highway,* where she writes a very moving account of the death of her Zen mentor, Dainin Katagiri Roshi, and describes the rituals that followed.[1]

One of those rituals was the opportunity to view his body for three days after he died as it lay in the *zendo* (meditation hall). Goldberg arrived at the end of the first day. She bowed and walked into the zendo and went over to the open coffin, which was a simple pine box. (The students had found one with a Jewish star on it and removed the star.) Goldberg writes, "I was forty-two years old and somehow had managed never to see a corpse. This was the first. I stood and looked. The zendo was dark, except for lit candles at the altar. There were many flowers. Roshi's skin looked dark and dry and he didn't move. I just stood there. The windows near the body were opened and the cruel March air of Minneapolis filled the space around him. . . ."

She visited his body the second and third days and observed some of the physical changes resulting from the natural processes of death. On the second day, in daylight, his skin looked yellow and tight. His features were sharper. On the third day, his skin had begun to shrink. His upper lip had lifted, and she could see part of his teeth.

On the fourth day, there was a short ceremony at the zendo. Then the coffin was closed and ceremoniously carried out by the monks to the hearse.

At the funeral home, they held a cremation ceremony. "The box was carried away by the disciples," Goldberg writes. "We all moved to a brown-carpeted waiting room, stood around, had tea and visited." The crematorium had allowed the monks to put the coffin in the oven, and one of the disciples turned on the gas to begin the burning. For the next several hours, Goldberg was aware of her teacher's body being burned. She went out to eat, then returned to the funeral home. "I walked down a long cement basement hall into a small cement room," she writes. "The door was heavy and hard to open. It was hot in that room and there was a ferocious constant noise: It was the oven."

She looked in the oven: "I opened the door of the oven and looked in. Through the heat and intense flames, I saw two small ribs—that was all. They were the last of my great teacher."

Throughout the burning, Roshi's disciples sat *zazen* (in meditation). In this way, they demonstrated their devotion and shared their grief in the context of their religious community. Their love poured into this space where they let go of his body.

I was surprised to read about this cremation ceremony, particularly the description of Goldberg opening the door to the oven as her teacher's body burned. I was also moved by this account of how Goldberg and her companions were able to express their devotion. Clearly, their hands-on rituals helped them express their love, feel their loss, and begin to let go.

More recently, consumer advocate Lisa Carlson has written about ways families can be more directly involved in preparing a body for its final committal.[2] She begins her book, *Caring for the Dead: Your Final Act of Love,* with her experience when her husband, John, committed suicide. Distraught with the funeral home's price tag of $700 for cremation, she investigated other options and found a crematory that would handle disposition of his body for $85. This involved transporting him herself, which she did with help from a friend. As a result of choosing this option for financial reasons, however, she discovered that being closely involved was "an overwhelming, therapeutic kind of experience."[3]

As Carlson points out, the funeral practices that protect family members from having direct involvement in death rituals are a relatively recent change and are peculiar to American culture. Visitors to the burning ghats (platforms) that line holy rivers in India, Nepal, and other countries where Hinduism is practiced will witness the practice whereby families not only burn the bodies of their loved ones but then smash the skull before sweeping the remains into the sacred waters of the river. Having observed this ritual in Nepal (and having seen the sorrow in the faces of family members), I cannot help but contrast it with the typical burial in American society where artificial grass and a steel-reinforced contraption conceal the grave and dirt is scarce or unavailable. Family and friends are escorted away before the casket is lowered. Every effort is directed toward sparing the family members any reminder that this is their final good-bye—the only one they will have. These practices that protect people from their grief and encourage control of emotions serve only to postpone it or repress it. This well-intentioned protection serves only to create a lot of business for therapists who assist people with working through their unresolved issues of grief.

As Lisa Carlson points out, many people are recognizing their needs to be more personally involved and are participating more proactively in planning for death rituals. My experience with funeral directors has been more positive than hers, perhaps because I have encountered cooperation when I have encouraged family participation. The funeral directors will not necessarily suggest that parents come in to dress a child for burial, for example, but they will accommodate almost anything that their clients request. It is helpful for families to have an advocate such as a minister, counselor, or friend—someone who will know the family's needs and be assertive about getting those needs honored.

TO DONATE OR NOT TO DONATE?

Florence was a kind and charitable person known for her generosity, compassion, and integrity. She was also an atheist with a pragmatic view of death. She had taken care to join a memorial society well in advance of her death and had signed legal papers offering her body to science. She instructed her family to hold no funeral or memorial services in her behalf and was pleased that she had spared them the trouble of having to deal with her remains. She knew they would have good memories of their time with her and albums full of photographs. Her chief legacy was in the thousands of students she had taught in her thirty-year career as a sixth-grade teacher and in her four wonderful children.

Her family carried out her wishes. It was several years later that I spoke with her son, whose grief had resurfaced in the form of anger at his mother. First, he was angry that she had given her body to a medical school without consulting with the family. More than that, however, he was angry that he had been denied the opportunity to offer a final good-bye. He was haunted by visions of parts of her body in pathology lab refrigerators or cremated piecemeal when their usefulness expired. He found out later that arrangements could have been made with the medical school to return the remains of her body for cremation, but it was too late.

This young man's grief had been exacerbated by a gesture of charity and integrity. We could not undo what had been done, but we could do what had not been done. Inviting several members of his family to a private memorial service, we gathered in his backyard for a simple ceremony of remembering—of sharing memories and, finally, of saying good-bye.

There are many people like Florence—people who want something good to come of their death. There are also many like her son, who was deprived of an opportunity to grieve. If you wish to donate your body to medicine, by all means discuss this decision with your family—preferably in the presence of a religious professional or counselor. Then become acquainted with all the options that might follow, and do not try to deprive your family of an opportunity to hold a ceremony of remembering and letting go.

Donating specific organs is a less complex issue, as it does not delay the opportunity to commit the body and does not evoke as many images of mutilation as the medical school scenario. It is a choice I have made for myself in my decision to put a designation on my driver's license that permits parts of my body to be removed if they are healthy enough for transplant to another human being.

Nevertheless, it is a decision that may evoke images of bodily intrusion that are troublesome to some members of the family or may conflict with their religious beliefs. Discussion with those who will have to live with the decision is, again, imperative.

At the risk of oversimplifying a complex matter, I want to offer a few summary statements regarding the process of making decisions after a death has occurred.

First, here is some advice as you consider the decisions you want made for your own death:

- Give some thought to what you wish to have done after you die. Do you want to donate your body or parts of it to science? Do you want your body cremated? Embalmed? Do you want to leave instructions for your memorial service?

- Discuss your wishes with your family. Consider their feelings and their spiritual perspectives as you communicate yours to them.

- Recognize that regardless of what you want, your family will need to grieve. Be willing to compromise or let go of your wishes if they are too emotionally difficult for your family to carry out.

- Do not request that there be no memorial service after you die. Let people know what you despise or find objectionable about memorial services, but do not deprive others of their need to remember and let go.

- Keep in mind that you do not have any control, really, over what happens after you are gone.

And here are a few words of advice for those who have to make the decisions after a family member has died:

- You must respect the intention of a person's wishes, but you must also care for your emotional needs and the needs of others who grieve.

- Participate as much as you can in the rituals of grieving. The more you love, the more you will hurt. Do not run away from the pain, for it will catch up with you later in subtle disguise and be more difficult to heal.

- The two most common ways people protect themselves from pain are by having no rituals at all and by following the customary traditions where euphemisms abound, embalming covers over death, dirt is scarce, and the funeral ends before the physical remains have been placed in their final resting place.

- Death is a natural process, part of our spiritual journey. So is grief. The better you are able to be present through your pain, the sooner you will be able to let go.

- You cannot undo what has been done in the past, but you can do what has not yet been done. It may be too late to change a decision that was made, but it is not too late to create a ritual that will help you address your current needs. This may be the memorial ceremony that never took place or a ritual that helps you let go of anger or guilt. (Suggestions for rituals that can be devised months or years after a death are offered in Chapter Nine.)

CHAPTER FIVE

Soul Sketch

Creating a Memorial Portrait

When you stop to think about it, the very idea of distilling the meaning of a person's life into a service that lasts about an hour is quite absurd. But that is not the purpose of a memorial service. Its purpose is to honor something of what it meant for that person to live. We are not there to summarize a person's life; we are there to honor the person's presence and offer witness to how he or she enriched us and our world. And we are there to say good-bye, knowing that we carry something of that person's spirit into our days of living.

Chapter Two discusses the issues that families face as they select speakers. Among those who offer tributes should be one person who can create a "soul sketch," a quickly but sharply drawn summation of a person's way of being in the world. It may be the only tribute offered, but more often it will be followed by the more personal remarks of people who knew the person well. It is they who can fill in the details of shading, putting a twinkle in the eye or a familiar gurgle into a burst of laughter.

The soul sketch describes dimensions of a person gleaned from conversations with several people, each of whom has a different experience. Thus the speaker who presents a soul sketch can describe the person's relationships from a more objective perspective. This portrait provides the setting for the personal remarks of others.

Most often it will be the person conducting the service who presents a soul sketch. For that reason, this chapter on memorial portraits is addressed primarily to individuals who will be trusted with creating a service of memory. In describing some principles that are essential to my processes, I hope that they will be helpful to those who feel equipped with the skills and sensitivities required for this task of interviewing families. Of course, some of the principles of writing a soul sketch are applicable to any offering of words in honor of someone who has died.

THE SOUL OF THE SKETCH

As the person offering a soul sketch, you are trusted with the task of honoring several dimensions of relationship. All human beings live in relationship to themselves, to nature, to other people, to the larger community of humans, and to their understanding of the transcendent, holy mysteries.

It is not enough to say that a man loved to fish. Why did he love it so? How did fishing feed his soul?

It is not enough to say that a child was kind to other children. How was her kindness an expression of her ethos—of her deeper relationship to life's purpose?

It is not enough to say that a woman achieved the highest distinction in her profession. What called her to devote her life to this endeavor?

It is not enough to say that a couple was happily married for sixty years. What principles of relationship nourished them through those years?

When I meet with members of a family, I ask a lot of questions. Some of them are pretty personal, and the answers may not belong in any public gathering. So why do I ask? Because a soul sketch will include a bit of shading, where the shadows add character and definition to the more notable features. Individual human beings deserve to be remembered for who they were, not who we wish they had been or who they were some of the time.

Even when you have known the person who died, you should spend at least two hours with members of the family. You will get better acquainted with the individual, seeing him or her through different eyes. If you have not ever seen the person you will honor, ask for photos or visit the home in order to get a feeling for who the person was. Throughout the planning of the service, this will help you keep that person's presence in your own heart.

THE INTERVIEW

Since people do not all have the same needs, no two interviews with members of bereaved families are ever the same. There are, however, common principles to apply to all conversations.

Tell the family members ahead of time that they will need to set aside two hours for your time together, and ask them to gather any materials that might be helpful in your planning. If you are meeting at their home, you may wish to ask them to refrain from answering the phone, either by having a friend or neighbor answer for them or by using an answering machine. The same friend can greet any visitors at the door and keep your time with the family free from intrusion. Since you are asking for two hours and this is an intense and emotional time, tell the family members to feel free to stand up or move as they need to, including trips to the bathroom. Be sure a box of tissues is placed in easy reach.

First, take some time (usually fifteen to thirty minutes) to hear how they are faring, and invite them to tell any stories that need to be told about this death and their initial feelings. Then set the tone for your planning. What you want to do at the service, you might say, is to make the person present, so you should ask them to do that for you now.

Certain questions are bound to come up during any family conference, and it is up to you whether or not you want to prepare a list in advance. I prefer to keep an interview open-ended, asking questions in a more spontaneous fashion as family members offer their comments and stories.

After your initial invitation to people to make the absent person present, they usually begin with adjectives. The first ones out of their mouths will generally be the person's most salient characteristics.

As they offer general remarks, ask for specifics. If they say a man had a great sense of humor, ask them to describe it or give examples. If they say a woman loved gardening, ask what her favorite plants were. If they say a little girl was very loving, ask how she expressed this love. In the back of your mind, try to form a picture of how the person related to self, others, and the holy mysteries of life.

What usually happens is that people in families play off of each other's comments and stories. Sometimes they offer very different perspectives and engage in significant dialogue with one another. I recall two brothers who had lost their mother. As the older son spoke about how his mother had always been there for him, the other said, "You got to have all her attention before she went to work; she wasn't there when I came home from school." I witnessed a beautiful exchange as the older brother took in and, perhaps for the first time, understood his brother's perspective. This older brother had also been very eager to speak; the younger one was far more reticent, speaking mostly in response to my asking, "And what about you, Earl? Does that describe your experience, too?" It was apparent that their mother had been a good mother to both sons, but "good mother" meant something different to each sibling.

As family members become more comfortable with sharing, both with you and with one another, you may sense that you can move a little deeper. A question you might ask when trust has developed is, "How did _____ express anger and affection?" Assure them, of course, that you do not wish to pry into their private life, and they do not need to feel pressured to answer any questions that are not comfortable for them. You will not include everything they say in your remarks at the service. What this question addresses, however, is at the heart of all relationships, and their responses will offer some insight into family relationships in particular.

Do not be afraid to ask if the person had any notable weaknesses. Since every human being has at least a few flaws, this gives the family permission to acknowledge them. You may or may not find a way to include this information in the sketch, depending on what they say. What is important is that you make space for acceptance of imperfection. It may be important for members of the family to express in this setting what cannot be said in a public gathering.

Another question that may come up is one that invites them to name the events in the person's life that shaped who he or she was. You do not need an entire life history, but if a man triumphed over polio as a young person or was orphaned at the age of six, it is important to know about it. This kind of information does not usually show up in the obituary. This often triggers remarks about how the person dealt with life's challenges and evokes descriptions of personal strengths and qualities—ambition, spirituality, reserve, determination, self-doubt, impatience, perfectionism, stubbornness, and so on.

If you are having difficulty getting a clear picture of what mattered to a person, you might ask questions like these: What did she like to read? What were his favorite activities? What kind of music did she enjoy? How did he relate to nature? What were her favorite possessions? When you remember him, where do you picture him (for example, in his favorite recliner, on the golf course, rummaging through the refrigerator)?

One of the questions you can ask, usually toward the end of your conversation, is, "What is _____'s chief legacy?" Even though the family may have already cited a number of proud accomplishments, this question will call up images of the lasting impressions the person made. It will get to the core of how family members think about the person and how the world will continue to benefit from the person's time on earth.

A good question to include and to ask of every member of the family is, "What will you miss most?" This question is really the most important, as it will evoke images of what has mattered in their relationships. Make sure the tissues are nearby, because this question will evoke a sense of loss. Death is separation, and the better the dead are remembered, the more they are missed. Also, the more they are missed, the better they are remembered.

It will probably take about an hour just talking about the person who died. Then for the last half hour or so, there is time to plan the service itself. If you need more time for this task, you can schedule it or plan to spend some time on the phone.

PLANNING THE SERVICE

As you plan the memorial or committal, you will need to explain different parts of the service (see Chapter Two) and encourage family participation. It is not unusual for them to say that they want to speak at the service but are not sure they will be able to handle it emotionally. So you can plan for them to have an out if they need it. This might be arranging for someone to read their written remarks or just checking in with them during the service in an unobtrusive manner. (Sometimes family members who say they do not want to speak at all will end up standing up to share memories or remarks when spontaneous remarks are invited.)

In many instances, you will not have the opportunity to speak with all members of a person's immediate family. When this is the case, ask for phone numbers so you can call them. Make a phone appointment ahead of time to be sure you will have an uninterrupted conversation for as long as is needed. Calling these family members is very important, as they will be traveling some distance to attend the memorial. After speaking with you, they will arrive feeling included, and if they did not know you before, now they have a personal connection.

You may want to suggest that the family create written materials for the service. A folder with a photograph and poetry or words of tribute is a keepsake for all who attend. It can also serve as a program offering information about speakers, music, and so on.

WRITING THE SOUL SKETCH

After your interview with a family, you have your scribbled notes from conversations and perhaps some supplemental materials such as newspaper articles or things written by the person who died. Now you must engage in your own creative process. It may help to begin with an organizing image.

Frequently, images and themes will speak through the lines of a poem. For example, for someone who was a thinker and a doer, there is a poem by S. Hall

Young that may fit. In the first stanza, the poet writes, "Let me die, working"; the second begins, "Let me die, thinking"; and the third begins, "Let me die, giving."[1]

Two poems that offer images for creating a portrait for someone who was intellectually curious, spiritually engaged, or whose life offered something of greatness to the world are "When Death Comes" by Mary Oliver and "Ailey, Baldwin, Floyd, Killens, and Mayfield" by Maya Angelou. The image of a life that has been a gift is expressed through May Sarton's poem, "All Souls."

Some people are not so easy to describe, for they are full of contradictions. The image of contradiction is expressed wonderfully in Walt Whitman's words, "Do I contradict myself? Very well, I contradict myself. I am large. I contain multitudes."[2] These lines were a point of departure for part of a soul sketch describing a brilliant young woman who was very overweight:

> Liza's physical largeness perhaps contributed to an inner largeness in which she contained contradictions. She could be shy in spite of her ability to have words for any occasion. She was tenderhearted and quick-tempered. She was rebellious and loving. She knew that her verbal talents could win honors or get her in trouble. She was gifted with intelligence and handicapped by frustration.

Most people contain multitudes, and it enhances a memorial tribute to describe them in terms of some of the tensions or contradictions in their lives.

Jerry Broidy, for example, was a man who could tickle anyone's funny bone, even if it was concealed under a stuffed shirt or a lofty title. Known for his lighthearted humor, he was also very serious about life and confronted injustice with remarkable moral courage. Schooled in the streets of the Bronx, he made his way from the boyhood scuffles of Fox Street, via the battlefields of Europe, to take his place among the most sophisticated contenders of Madison Avenue.

Although he had abandoned his Jewish religion, he taught and lived by the Hebrew phrase *tikkun ha'olam,* which means "to repair, reorder, or heal the world." Those who knew him well knew he was incisive, cantankerous, and quick to judge. He was also gentle, generous, and quick to forgive. If he did not always offer understanding, he was always accepting. He fancied himself a curmudgeon and could raise his voice in an impressive New Yorker display of anger. He also remembered the words of a ninety-year-old woman he met in a museum one day when he was hot and tired. Admiring her energy, he asked her how she managed to live so long. "Oh, it's easy my dear," she said. "I forgive everybody everything."

The soul sketch of Jerry, then, included a description of these characteristics as well as brief stories of how he lived his values in the world of relationships.

Noting the contradictory qualities of a person can also evoke smiles or laughter. This was the case with Ricardo, a young man who died at the age of twenty-nine. Very heavily into physical fitness, he followed his workouts with Coke, Doritos, and candy bars. Fastidious about careful advance planning in his profession, he did all his Christmas shopping on Christmas Eve. Protective of others, he would risk his own life and limb to prove he could accomplish something.

Sometimes a metaphor will emerge from the materials and conversations about a person's life, and the metaphor provides a theme for the sketch. Cynthia, for example, was a dancer whose life ended tragically in an automobile accident. The image of the dance (and of her favorite flower, the sunflower) suited this young woman, who offered a natural breezy but very engaged presence. She knew how to laugh at herself but was not self-deprecating; she sought out the goodness in others but was no Pollyanna. She could see the evil in the human heart, but she was no cynic. Throughout her life she stepped—or rather danced—to the beat of a different drummer. Her life dance also expressed a sensual aesthetic spirituality. Whether she was dancing or gardening, arranging flowers or weaving images into a quilt, she embodied spirit, and her ability to heal with a touch of her hands (as a massage therapist) was an expression of her being in step with the rhythms of life.

For William, who was a builder and contractor, the sketch picked up on the images of construction to describe some of his personal characteristics. His steady loving companionship was a foundation for his family life; his tendency toward a modest frugality was affectionately referenced as an aversion to Victorian "gingerbread"; his curiosity and love for the natural world translated into a respect for the landscape and careful attention to "constructing" a life compatible with its setting.

The language of home and garden provides images for many people. For example, a woman who loved to garden planted and nurtured seeds of love and caring in the souls of her children, receiving her greatest satisfaction from seeing the fruits of her labor. She had been inclined to overdo her nurture at times, but it was her loving intentions, not her fretful pruning, that dominated their memory of her, and they had thrived in her presence.

Music is of course a theme for many people, and a song often provides the images for a soul sketch.

It was a traditional Shaker song, "Simple Gifts," chosen by the family of Jane Melkonian, that organized the soul sketch for her service.[3] The entire sketch is presented here to demonstrate the virtue of simplicity in writing memorial portraits as well as in living life. Perhaps you have been fortunate enough to know someone like Jane.

'Tis a gift to be simple, to be grounded in values of honesty, integrity, and love.

'Tis a gift to be free, to know and accept yourself, to be free from striving for material things, to know what is most important in life.

'Tis a gift to come down where you ought to be, to be content with life, to delight in times with family and friends, to offer something good into the world every day.

This was Jane's gift.

She was remarkably strong in character but not overbearing; she was competent, self-contained, and self-confident at the same time that she was modest. She was humble without being self-effacing.

Jane had a gift of creating space for the human spirit to grow, to bond with others, and to connect with the rhythms of love and beauty that give life its meaning. She could fill you up with a smile.

It was a gift imbued with affection, with integrity.

And with humor. She delighted in observing human folly, but innately kind and generous, she was never one to make fun of others.

Simple gifts. These are the gifts Jane gave to Al through years of marriage, and to Steve, Jim, and Tom, as she made their home a loving and growing place.

These were the gifts she offered to friends who knew they were valued, appreciated, accepted, and respected in her presence.

These were the gifts she gave in the community, where she volunteered her time generously.

These were the gifts she gave to us here in our religious community, where she reached out to others and made deep, caring connections with friends.

These were the gifts she gave to people she worked with at the high school, feeling enriched by them as she encouraged them and took genuine interest in their lives. I suspect she trained many a principal without their even realizing they were being trained.

It was Jane's nature to offer her gifts, never to impose them. With an aesthetic sense that permeated every part of her life and a simple grounding in what really matters, Jane was unpretentious—so much so that she was not conscious of being unpretentious, if you know what I mean. In this way she also lived with a grace rooted in spiritual depth. She did not articulate her spiritual nature—she just lived it.

Consistent with this, she was responsive, not intrusive; she was discerning and perceptive, wise and strong. She did not waste time on disappointment, blame, or regret. Easing slowly into social situations, she engaged fully once into them.

Jane lived according to strongly held values. You knew what they were, and you knew without her saying it when you weren't living up to them. Jane voiced her opinions clearly, but not judgmentally. She served her ideals in her everyday living, in her regard for people, in her respect for the gifts of nature. It was a natural extension of her deep sense of connection with others that she considered how it felt to be in someone else's shoes. Thus she reached out in compassion to others, whether it was to a beloved member of her family or to a stranger at the shelter for homeless families.

'Tis a gift to be simple, to be free, to come down where you ought to be. As I met with Al, Steve, Jim, and Tom, I asked them what they felt was Jane's legacy in the world. "You're looking at it" was the reply, not with a hint of personal pride, but with a deep awareness of how her values were lived into their lives and hearts and are there always. She taught her sons to leave a place better than they found it. She leaves this world better for having lived in it.

As they speak now of this beloved wife and mother, her legacy is clear to us all.

In the tragedy *Hamlet*, the young prince ponders aloud to his friend Horatio on the topic of death. "There is special providence in the fall of a sparrow," says Hamlet. "If it be now, 'tis not to come; if it be not to come, it will be now; if it be not now, yet it will come. The readiness is all."

The readiness is all.

Shakespeare reminds us that we don't have a lot of control over when or how we will die. Where we do have some say, however, is in how we live. Our readiness is less a readiness to die than a readiness to live fully and meaningfully; that way we are more ready for death.

So I have been imagining that my husband Chuck is sitting in some minister's study, joined perhaps by other family members. The minister has read my book and is asking some of the questions that I have asked.

To be honest, I recoil from the thought, but I force my imagination for the sake of practicing what I preach.

My attention turns, however, not to what I want in my memorial service but how I will be remembered. I think less of what I want at death and more of what I want in my life, particularly in my relationships—with self, with others, and with the Spirit that gives purpose to it all. Although I am writing this book about memorial rituals, I have very little instruction for those who will remember me. I just know I want them to do it well, for the sake of their own grieving. I want them to be honest, even if it means that words like *impatience* or (dread the thought) *control* get mentioned in some connection with me. I want to know that I was accepted and loved for who I was, appreciated for what I gave, and remembered through their own ways of living and being.

If there is one thing I would like to give to each person who reads this book, it is readiness. I do not mean readiness to die by having things "in order," even though there is wisdom in that. I mean readiness to live, so that when death comes, you will be remembered well.

CHAPTER SIX
All Deaths Are Not Equal

The Many Faces of Death

IT WAS EARLY SEPTEMBER, AND RICKY, SIXTEEN YEARS OLD, WAS ON THE WAY to school on his new motorcycle. "Be careful," his mother admonished as he rushed out the door. "Don't worry, Mom," he smiled, with an irresistible and convincing blend of charm and affection.

That was the last time she would see Ricky alive. No one could tell him he wasn't immortal as he tested his new bike on roads still wet with dew. Going too fast for conditions, he slid and collided with a dumpster.

The memorial service was four days later. Sitting in the front pew of the church were Ricky's parents and his younger sister, Laura. Only a few weeks before, his mother and father had argued about whether or not Ricky should have a motorcycle. He had completed a recovery program for drug addiction and had been drug-free for almost a year, but his mother was nervous. "He is buying it mostly with his own money," said his father. "And he is sixteen. You can't tell him to act like an adult and treat him like a child."

The minister planning the service knew enough of the family circumstances to be aware that Ricky's mother was trying hard not to blame her husband, who heaped plenty of blame on himself. And Ricky. How could he be so reckless? He had promised to be careful. His mother was angry, more angry than she could even say, at her young son's recklessness and at herself for somehow not being able to protect him against every harm. Ricky's sister, Laura, only eight years old, was also feeling bad because she had told Ricky she "hated" him and she had not had a chance to say she didn't mean it. All three of them were having a very hard time accepting Ricky's sudden death. So, too, were his classmates, whose grief was not only the loss of their classmate but also a shattering of their world of youthful promise.

How would the words of the memorial service hold a space for the feelings of Ricky's father, mother, and sister? How would the service address the feelings of the students and teachers from the school?

Very carefully—that's how. A memorial observance is not a therapy session. Neither is it a formulated ceremony where circumstances and the feelings they evoke can be ignored. The service that meets the needs of those who grieve the loss of a ninety-five-year-old who died peacefully after a short illness will not serve as well for parents who have abruptly lost a child.

No memorial service can address all the feelings that people bring with them. It can, however, hold those feelings in holy space and in the context of community, which is something that cannot be done in a thousand therapy sessions. To hold a space for feelings does not necessarily mean that you need to name every loss or anger or betray the privacy of those who gather. It means only what it says—there is space in which the feelings are honored and safe.

Also, it is essential that anyone who takes responsibility for holding that space does so with a sense of what is appropriately public or private, working with families to ascertain their level of comfort. In situations where death is violent, self-inflicted, or made more complex because of family alienation, a trained professional should be consulted. Clergy of all faiths are generally the most experienced, but others, particularly some therapists, are also trained and skilled in crafting sensitive memorials.

The minister who met with Ricky's family was aware, as he prepared for the memorial service, of feelings he wanted to honor. High school teachers and classmates packed the sanctuary for the service. Members of the twelve-step group that had supported Ricky through his struggles with drug addiction also attended. After an initial greeting, acknowledging those gathered, the minister said:

> This warm day protests the end of summer. So, too, we come in protest to Ricky's unseasonable death, hoping that in these sacred moments of remembering, we may come closer to accepting the unacceptable and finding meaning where there is no meaning.
>
> How could it be that we are here without Ricky today? Just a few days ago he was at football practice and joking with Mr. Taylor about having to put up with him in English class again. Only last Saturday he was mowing the lawn and singing along with the music on his earphones. It seems like yesterday that he was sitting at the dinner table teasing his little sister and sneaking scraps to the dog under the table.
>
> How could it be that he is gone? Just like that. How is it we will not hear him laugh or be able to kid him about his terrible jokes? How can it be that this young man who was finally getting his life together will not have a chance to live into his adult years? How is it we will not have one more chance to tell him we love him and get one more of his wonderful affectionate hugs?

These questions gnaw at us in the wake of Ricky's sudden death. There are no easy answers. Although Ricky died too young and in the fullness of his youth, we may derive some consolation in our knowledge that he struggled through painful times and emerged triumphant. His strength was in his gentleness. His youthful wisdom was earned courageously. Fearless and, yes, reckless, he tested the limits of living and loving. In his death as well as his life, he charges you to love him *as he was*.

The minister did not feel it necessary to talk about Ricky's struggle with addiction or name the nature of the anger many felt. (At another point in the service, someone recited the serenity prayer that is used in twelve-step meetings.) What he wanted to do was to acknowledge that Ricky had a self-destructive tendency, to make room for the anger people were feeling, and to open the way for remembering him well.

When young people have lost a classmate, no matter how death occurred, a memorial service should include them. At Ricky's service, a teacher spoke, and some of Ricky's friends offered their tribute to him with a song.

Automobile accidents often involve other people who may be injured or be feeling guilty or angry, depending on why the accident occurred. These individuals may not be able to attend a memorial service. If they cannot attend, it should be noted in the opening remarks. If very close family members are absent, it might be mentioned that they will receive a tape of the service. Of course, as technology advances, the time will soon come when they will be able to tune in through electronic connections.

The best place to make space for their feelings is in a prayer. For example, a young woman was with her boyfriend when she was killed in an automobile accident. Her boyfriend was in the hospital with a broken shoulder and could not attend the service. In the prayer, after invoking support for those who grieved the loss of this young woman, the minister said, "We name also Chad, whose visible wounds and wounds of grief need healing. Not only has he lost his beloved Julia, but also he cannot be here to share this time of mourning and remembering with us."

In another situation where a person (the driver, who had been drinking) was injured in an accident where there were two fatalities, she was conscious enough to write a statement and have it read at the funeral of one of the people who died. Not only did this help her own process of grieving, but it was also a gift to the many people who cared for her. She was a courageous young woman who asked the minister to name her in the prayer and pray that God would forgive her. The request for prayer was not only her desire for divine mercy, it was an invitation to others to hear her sorrowful regret. It opened the door to the conversations and prayers that might eventually enable them to forgive her for what she could not change.

Young people are not the only ones to die in accidents, of course. Randall, a man in his fifties, was hit by a car while riding his bicycle. The driver of the car was not speeding or driving recklessly. But Randall was riding on a road where visibility was not good. If anyone were to be blamed, it was Randall. But blame was not on the agenda, just loss. During the opening remarks for his service, I said, "Randall's accident was an abrupt and unnatural end. The day of his accident, he was training for a biking tour next month in England—something he had been looking forward to for years. We come today feeling the loss of this unfulfilled dream as well as our own loss. We are stunned by his untimely death."

It was probably my own need as much as anyone's to offer a prayer for the person who, according to the newspaper report, was driving the car that was in the wrong place at the wrong time. During a prayer late in the service, I named the driver among those we held in our hearts, saying, "We offer also a prayer of compassion for Bud, whose car dealt the fatal blow, for he too carries a burden of pain and grief unlike any other." A few days later, I received a note from Bud, thanking me for the prayer. I did not know he had attended the service.

DEATH BY CHOICE

There are few people whose lives have not been touched by suicide. The first time I conducted a memorial for a person who chose death, I became aware of how important it is to name the circumstances of suicide and make space for the feelings that accompany that. I did not know the woman who chose to die, and I did not know any of her family. They had received my name from someone at the funeral home.

Jodie was a physician in her forties—a bright, successful woman who had mothered two children and appeared to have everything to live for. Twice married and twice divorced, she lived alone.

I spent several hours with her family—or I should say families. After speaking with her former husband, it was clear that I needed to meet separately with her children (from her first marriage). A third group consisted of some other relatives who wanted their own session as well. After about six hours of conversation, I felt I had become acquainted with Jodie—so well, in fact, that after the service, several of her friends and relatives asked how long I had known her. They were astounded that we had never met. The fact was, I had gotten to know this woman because the nature of her death required more of me. It required more of all of us.

Included in my opening remarks, I offered some statements about Jodie's choice and made room for some of the feelings it evoked.

We come into this time with a range of emotions as deep and complex as the woman we are remembering.

Here there is love—and the searing pain of separation.

Here there is anger—and the futile search to understand why Jodie could not weather the despair that locked her alone into her self.

Here there are questions—why, mostly. Why?

Some of you come feeling bruised by this death and asking what you might have done to prevent it.

Jodie's choice to die touches the despair that courts many of us in our own moments of loneliness and threatens the structures of meaning that affirm our own lives. Let us remember that no single act of desperation can define a life. No matter how stalked by pain, Jodie's life also had its moments of delight and happiness, caring and friendship, sharing and love. Death by choice is not a denial of life; it is the cry of despair for more life. It grows from a deep personal alienation or profound suffering and is carried out alone, after a struggle within the self.

When a death such as this cuts across life in its fullness, we are left with a certain incompleteness. We know that Jodie leaves much unfinished, unfulfilled, unsaid. There are still other things you wanted to share with her and she with you: Graduations, weddings, the birth of grandchildren; another walk on the beach at sunset with Justin, another shopping spree with Ellen, another bridge game with the club. This sadness for the loss of this life, full and blossoming, mingles with the sadness for the loss of possibilities not realized.

The effect of my having said these things was remarkably liberating for those who gathered. There is something heavy and burdensome about entering a room where everyone is thinking about something but it is never spoken. The power of the unmentionable subject to tinge both the living and the dead with a subtle shame is defused when it can be named.

It was several years later that I would experience these same issues from the perspective of the bereaved instead of the minister. It was at the memorial service for my stepson, who chose to end his life at the age of twenty-eight. I had known and loved him for twenty-seven of those years.

I spoke with Tom on the last day of his life, only minutes before I rushed off to the airport to catch a plane for a conference on the Caribbean island of St. John. By the time my husband, Chuck, was able to reach me (it was a very long and circuitous trip adapted to routes available on frequent-flier credits), Tom had been dead for twenty-four hours. By the time I was able to arrange another flight back to North Carolina, where Tom and his wife lived, the minister, Janet Harvey, had already met with the rest of the family. She requested time to meet with me alone, which was very helpful, but I went to the service with a sense of being a little on the outside of things. (I was perhaps more sensitive to this exclusion because I was a stepparent.) By the time the minister had offered her opening remarks, however, I felt that she had opened a circle to hold my feelings as well as those of Tom's birth parents and his wife. All of us were relieved that she could name Tom's choice with respect for his human struggle and also with understanding for our difficulty accepting the finality of his actions. After her initial greeting, she said, "We gather to honor Tom's memory and to support one another in grieving a death that is the hardest death to grieve: death that is chosen."

She offered a prayer and then said:

On Sunday morning, Tom completed a decision. Where there is pain and confusion, despair and doubt, we long for the end to suffering. For some, like Tom, life no longer has any choices but one. Life left scars that Tom could not find the inner resources to heal. The inner pain was too great—pain that he had contained within himself for years, pain that often lashed out in anger, mostly at himself. Tom chose to end the suffering for himself. The mind was exhausted, the heart frightened, and the end taken. The suffering does not end, however, for those who have loved and cared for him. Friends and family are left with feelings of shock, betrayal, anger, sadness, and—in time—compassion and forgiveness.

Those who are left ask and continue to ask, "What could I have done? Why didn't I see it?"

No one knows. And nothing will bring him back.

No one is responsible for Tom's choice but Tom.

A VIOLENT DEATH

Like suicide, a death that results from a violent attack evokes a sense of tragedy and horror. There is often an element of public grieving as well. This was certainly the case when the story of Peggy's brutal stabbing and beating spread throughout the small town where she lived. I was shocked to read that her three young children had been in the house, where they could hear the blows, the screams, and the silence as their father murdered their mother.

Peggy's other relatives lived in another state, and they planned to hold a private ceremony there. But Peggy's closest friends and coworkers needed a memorial service that would honor the dignity and spirit of their friend. They were the ones who met with me to help create the service.

Peggy was a very private person, but her memorial service was anything but private. Camera crews from the local TV station arrived to tape the memorial and stayed respectfully and unobtrusively in the balcony. The pews filled with women who had not known Peggy but knew how it felt to live in fear of an abusive spouse or partner. Many people came because Peggy's death had touched something tender in them, and they wanted to join in this gathering where we would honor her valiant spirit and bless her bruised soul.

Peggy's protection of her privacy was so great, in fact, that few of her closest companions were aware of how much she suffered. Wanting to be respectful of her privacy at the same time that I wanted to create a caring space for people who gathered, I offered these words in my opening remarks, after an initial greeting:

> Some of you did not know Peggy, but you come in the wake of her tragic death to honor her life. Friends and strangers to one another, you create a community that includes not only those present but also family and friends who are not here today, particularly Peggy's children, Alan, Katy, and Kurt, and their grandparents, whose grief is compounded beyond what any of us can know. It includes also her husband, Rob, whose grief is his own doing and undoing; who carries an unknowable loss in his own soul.
>
> We who gather here today come feeling heavy with a sense of brokenness and tragedy. We carry it for a community that has lost a fair and youthful spirit full of goodness. We carry it for Peggy's friends and family. We carry it especially for her children. Haunted by images of unspeakable violence, we come to invite the spirit of peace into Peggy's life and memory.
>
> Some of you carry your own personal sense of regret that you did not do something to prevent her death. Tomorrow evening there will be a vigil where the community may confess its collective guilt, pain, or anger for Peggy and for other women who have suffered in relationships where love has gone astray. Evoking the redemptive power of hope, that will be an occasion

for community empowerment. This evening, however, we come not to hold up the tragedy and ugliness of Peggy's death but to honor the beauty and love in her life. This is not a time to speculate about her suffering but to witness to the courage it took for her to carry on her life with dignity.

It is important to name the circumstances of a violent death and to make space for the anger and guilt that people feel, but it is even more important not to allow a brutal death to violate the memories we hold up as we honor a life. Later in the service, I sketched a memorial portrait of this young woman who was most of all a devoted mother, then closed with the following:

> Peggy was a very private person who kept her home life quite separate from work. Outside of her family, few people knew of her suffering or her fears or her hopes for change. It would be a betrayal of the personal dignity and courage she maintained to speculate about this part of her life that has become so public in her death. It would also be irresponsible to attempt to construct the truth of a life from general assumptions, stereotypes, and rumor. It is enough to say that she made several attempts to become free, and her love and hope drew her back as a moth is drawn to a flame. It appears that she was packed and truly about to leave the only home she knew. A young woman with the courage to endure, she also had the courage to become free. Thus it is that while her death was tragic, she left this world with an inner freedom and a noble heart. She is free, and we pray that her spirit may be embraced by the peace and light of eternal rest.

It was my choice to include Rob in a spoken prayer later in the service:

> We pray also for Rob, whose violent deed will never be undone. For the sake of his children, his sister, Arlene, and his parents, we dare to pray that his life can be redeemed through the power of grace as well as the process of justice.

I chose to offer this prayer because of my own personal belief that we humans have the capacity to respond with hatred or with love to a person who has committed a despicable crime. In addition to acknowledging rage and calling for justice, I wanted to invoke the power of love, which does not spring from reason or logic and so does not always make sense. I felt particularly sad for Rob's parents and sister, who must have felt betrayed and ashamed at the same time they mourned Peggy's death.

A memorial service will not dilute anger or salve guilt or accomplish justice for wrongdoing. It is not the place to hold up a person as a saint or sinner. It is an occasion to allow the feelings to be what they are and to summon the power of the Holy to heal and comfort those who grieve. More than that, it is an opportunity to affirm those things that are most threatened by death and by the agents of death: to declare the triumph of love, freedom, and hope; to know there is possibility for change, to believe in the promise of new life and ultimate meaning. In all religious traditions, there are poetic and scriptural resources for evoking compassion **and** hope. In Jewish or Christian tradition, there are familiar scriptural passages such as Psalm 23 or 1 Corinthians 13 that articulate a theology of hope and grace, redemption and transformation.

SOME GENERAL GUIDELINES FOR UNTIMELY DEATH

As the foregoing examples illustrate, there are a few general guidelines that can be gleaned for planning funeral or memorial ceremonies when death is sudden, violent, self-inflicted, or untimely.

- Always name the circumstances, but do not allow them to overshadow the primary purpose of the service, which is to honor the person's life.

- There will be shock and denial—a sense, as Shakespeare put it, that time is "out of joint." Acknowledge that something about the order of things as we expect them to occur has been betrayed.

- Provide space for feelings of guilt, understanding that these feelings are not always rational or valid in terms of placing "blame" for a death.

- Provide space for feelings of anger—with self, with others, and with the Holy as you would name it.

- Know that there are unfinished conversations. Provide a time during the service for people to consider what they might have said if they had had one more opportunity.

- Choose words, readings, and prayers that will offer hope in the face of despair, redemption in the presence of evil, and transformation in spite of brokenness. Do not offer these, however, without acknowledging how much they are needed at this time when things have fallen apart.

WHEN AN INFANT DIES

Once in a while, I encounter people who teach me about spiritual power in ways that surprise and humble me. Michael Comando and Nanette True were two such people.

Michael and Nanette had just given birth to their first child, Avery—a baby so severely handicapped by a genetic defect that he was entirely dependent on machines to keep him alive. They had already made the choice to try to save his life, in spite of the knowledge that even if he lived, he would continue to be severely handicapped physically and mentally, requiring an incredible commitment from them. The nature of the infant's problems was such that medical personnel were not obligated by law to take lifesaving measures. Avery's parents, however, never had to think about it. They beheld a precious human being, their first child. Because they were able to love their child so totally and unconditionally, others, including me, were drawn into their circle of hope and could see what they were able to see.

Avery's little body failed to respond to the surgeries and treatments offered, and he died seven months after he was born. He was not just a handicapped infant who never had a chance, however; he was a person who had spent some time in this world, and his parents needed to hold a service to remember him well.

My remarks were specific to this family's context but could be adapted for any occasion of infant death. Using the format for the introduction described in Chapter Two, I offered a greeting and then said:

> On this autumn morn, we meet in space that is made sacred with the spirit of love and memory. For we have gathered here today to give testimony to the power of the brief life that Avery had on this earth: We gather also to mourn Avery's death, to say good-bye to him, and to commit his spirit to eternal peace.
>
> We gather first to remember Avery—to remember him in his helplessness and pain, yes—but to remember him also in his moments of infant delight: to recall his first smile and his growing response to the people around him.
>
> We gather also to mourn—to mourn for the loss of love growing into tomorrow, deepening and maturing through joy and conflict; to mourn for the empty spaces in a home that has been prepared so that he might take his place among family; to mourn for the opportunities Avery will not have to smell a flower, to walk in the snow, to play at the shore.
>
> Our tears of sadness for the loss of this new life cut short before it could blossom forth in fullness mingle with tears of sadness for the loss of hopes not realized.

With the sadness of loss, we come also in gratitude, thankful for the gifts of love and humanity that Avery gave to all who were touched by his valiant struggle; thankful for the difference he has made in the lives of so many who invested their skills and their hearts in the effort to keep him with us; thankful for the power of love that issued from his very being.

Thus, with tears of memory, of loss, and of gratitude, we are here to grow through an ending into a beginning—to let go of Avery and, with memories and treasures gathered up for the journey, gain strength for moving through the days ahead.

After a reading from *The Little Prince* chosen by the parents, I said:

"All of us must lose our hearts to a child. . . ."

I spoke with Michael and Nanette shortly after Avery was born, and it was clear to me then that they had already lost their hearts to this child who, though he had to depend on machines for his breath and life, was born with stardust in his hair, a holy and precious gift. He was their little prince, and no degree of physical brokenness diminished the devotion they poured out for him.

The story of Avery's short life is a story of love, a story of courage, a story of faith, a story of hope.

He knew more pain in his little body than most of us experience in an ordinary lifetime. It took most of his energy just to stay alive. Yet he could respond to the loving eyes of his mother and father or the caring touches received from his army of hospital attendants with a smile, a gurgle, or his own silent laughter. He could also let out a good angry belt when he'd had enough of being a pin cushion. As Nanette and Michael and other family and friends loved Avery into this world, he responded with remarkable strength and courage.

Avery's story is also a story of human possibility. Undaunted by the sterile barriers of hospital procedures, Nanette and Michael nurtured Avery, giving him what no surgery, tube, or injection could provide. To them, and to the others who worked so hard to keep him alive, Avery was not just a helpless, handicapped infant—he was a human being. They saw past the helpless patient to the boy.

So there were many who got acquainted with this little prince, who lost their hearts to him, who will remember him not only for who he was but for what he gave to them.

During the prayer, I offered these words:

Daily we are touched by the rhythms of life and death, yet now we are out of rhythm, for birth and death have seized too closely on the same moment. In sadness for the hopes that are not realized for Avery, we seek peace and hope. Disappointed that the fight for life has ended in death, we rest in the relief and assurance that Avery is liberated from pain and suffering.

DEATH BEFORE BIRTH

When a fetus is miscarried, aborted, or born dead, hospital personnel call this a "fetal demise." They know also that for whatever period of time, and with whatever circumstances of loss, a mother carried a child in her womb. Whether her pregnancy was for two months or nine, she lived in relationship with that child as well as with the father or others who participated in the hopes, plans, and decisions that were made for the life growing within her.

Health professionals are generally sensitive to the need for parents and family to express their grief. At some local hospitals, they encourage parents to hold a dead infant, and they take photographs of the body. The film is given to the parents, who choose whether or not to develop it. The parents receive a card with a stamp of the footprints and a keepsake box that contains a gown and cap and blanket. If the fetus has developed for fewer than twenty weeks, the hospital will cremate the body and give the parents the remains or release the fetus for private burial. (If the fetus has developed twenty weeks or more, the body is released according to the same laws that apply to other deaths.)

The footprints and the keepsake box can then be used for the ritual of committing the bodily remains. This was the case for the parents of a boy child who was developing with no brain; his life ended with a medically indicated abortion. On a table prepared for the ceremony, they laid the infant's ink footprints, a small carved box containing the infant's fetal remains, and a large blue candle. The candle was not lit, and it remained unlit for the short memorial. The unlit candle, a palpable symbol of a life never lived, offered a space for grief—an empty space bereft of the hopes for new life.

SOME GENERAL GUIDELINES
FOR INFANT OR FETAL DEATH

Drawing from the illustrations in this chapter and the example in Chapter One, there are some things to consider when you are planning ceremonies of memory for babies who die before or shortly after birth.

- Whether or not the child has breathed or been given a name, he or she *lived*. The child miraculously developed uniqueness and existed in relationship as a human being, not an "it."

- The death of an infant or fetus is often the death of the hopes and dreams of the parent or parents. Those hopes and dreams should be named.

- The physical remains, even of a fetus that has been aborted by choice, deserve a ceremony of committal. This honors not only the human life that developed in the mother's womb but also the relationship that existed between parent or parents and fetus. A ceremony will help bring closure to that relationship.

- To gather in community for a ceremony of memory and committal not only honors the brief life of the child but also gives social recognition to the depth of the loss of the parents. It is an invitation to others to recognize the family's grief and offer comfort.

WHEN ILLNESS IS A PLAYER

Sadie had Alzheimer's disease. For several years, she lived at home with her husband, George, who did his best to take care of her. As the disease advanced, he found a residential care center for her. He visited her daily until his own health problems made that difficult. With help from his daughter, he visited Sadie every week or so. By the time Sadie died, most people had not seen her for about five years. She had been active in her community, and the family wanted to create the opportunity for people who had been enriched by Sadie's life to attend her memorial. What the family did not realize is how much they needed to hear what others had to say. They had been losing Sadie little by little for a long time, and their loss made it difficult for them to remember who she was before the disease ravaged her mind. The people who came with their images of the Sadie they knew offered the family a gift at the same time that they were able to grieve for this person, whom they had not seen for a long time. Early in the service, the minister acknowledged the circumstances of Sadie's death:

After years of gradually losing Sadie and living with the pain of seeing her lose herself, we are now able to reach back to remember her as she was before Alzheimer's began to steal her away. Grief has come in stages through these years of her illness, but death is a final letting go. . . .

There was no need to say more, except to include the members of George's Alzheimer's support group in the prayer and to talk about how Sadie managed to be herself in many ways in spite of what her illness stole from her. "You'll have to take me in the present moment," she had said. And they did.

AIDS is another disease that writes the final chapter of a person's life and calls on family members (or extended family) to offer special care while they witness unspeakable suffering and anticipate their own loss. AIDS has devastated communities, changed whole cultures, and claimed many lives of young and creative people. It has also forced families into intimate space where they have experienced the heights and depths of emotion. Those who have suffered with this disease have become well acquainted with their own angels and demons. So have those who companioned them through their last years or months of life. How people with AIDS live through their suffering is the final chapter of their life story. It has also been a significant chapter in the life stories of those who companioned them.

Although the majority of Americans who have died from AIDS have been gay men, this disease can strike anyone, young or old, male or female, and it is now spreading faster among the nongay population. There is no formula for approaching a ceremony for someone who has died of AIDS, but anyone who plans for a service should be sensitive to some potential dynamics.

First is the shame factor. The most common way of contracting HIV (the virus that causes AIDS) is through sexual contact that results in an exchange of bodily fluids; the second most common transmission is by sharing needles for the injection of illegal drugs. In either case, there is the possibility of an element of social judgment on a person's sexual history or use of drugs. People will make assumptions, whether accurate or not. Even people who have contracted the virus as a result of a blood transfusion live under the cloud of shame that prompts them to explain how their blood was contaminated.

There is nothing constructive in the shame factor, and anything that you can do to help dispel it will contribute toward an honest and meaningful rite of death. Here are a few suggestions:

- Encourage openness about the cause of death. Not mentioning it says, in effect, that shame has been legitimized. This doesn't have to be in words. Some people say very little, but they display an AIDS Memorial Quilt piece or distribute red ribbons for people to wear during the service.

- Combat the religious or social associations of AIDS with illicit or unconventional sexual behavior by celebrating the positive and loving aspects of intimate relationship.

- Do not give in to the temptation to explain how someone did *not* acquire AIDS. This only serves to reinforce the notion of shame by association.

Second, there is almost always a story to be told about how this disease has affected a person's relationships. Be aware of the family dynamics. Particularly in the families of gay men, relationships have been shattered and healed as a result of dealing with HIV and AIDS. When Jesse, for example, was diagnosed with AIDS, he had not seen his parents for ten years—ever since he had announced that he was gay and moved in with Stanley. The story of his reconciliation with his father and his parents' devotion to him during his illness was a moving tribute to them all. When Carl was diagnosed, his parents did not know he was gay. As a result of being forced to come out, he experienced a loving acceptance from his Catholic parents that he had not expected—a true gift of grace for him in the midst of his physical torment. Quentin's story was the opposite, however. His family, upon learning of his illness, shut him out of their lives, and it was his extended family of close friends who took care of him. In each case, the illness and its impact on relationships was a significant final chapter of a life.

As a minister, Mark Belletini has seen many people face death; as a gay man, he has mourned the deaths of some of his closest friends. When his dear friend Stephen died, Mark offered a loving tribute of reminiscences from many chapters of Stephen's life. After offering images of Stephen as a young child, a youth, and a young man, Mark offered glimpses into the adult life of this man who was the only male in his college home economics department—who designed clothes, baked apple pies for dinner, and crafted furniture. Mark recalled Stephen "play-acting in zany and racy skits on the leather stage and being photographed by cameras that loved his amazing mustache and his beefy shoulders."

Although most of Mark's tribute was of Stephen, healthy and young, mounted on a Harley or maneuvering a kayak—playful prankster and serious student of life—Mark did not neglect to describe Stephen's final chapter as well:

> I see Stephen receiving the news that he has seroconverted, and I remember myself sobbing that day far from where he could hear me. Stephen, painfully watching friends like Coulter die before him, decides to plumb his inner life, poring over whole libraries of psychology and spirituality, devouring tapes of lectures and lyrics. He calls me incessantly, asking me questions both symbolic and direct about mortality, which I cannot of course answer except in

the language of mystery and poetry. He crafts collages of preternatural beauty—it's a kind of "diary of my dying," he tells me once. And he suffers, suffers more than anyone I have ever known. Meningitis, Stephens-Johnson syndrome, Kaposis purpling his arms and chest, a massive heart attack, and many other horrors that wrack the great soul and powerful body. Always he fights, always he wins more time—time to stage art shows to raise money for HIV charities; time to work out financial arrangements; time to play with his computer, which he trained almost like a pet; time to become closer to his parents, to his family, Mike and Lucy and Paula and so many others, and people as lucky as I, and to his dear Richard; time to go to the Gay Games as photographer; time to go to a wedding in New York City; time to attend *Angels in America* with Richard and me; time to write letters, to organize, and even, from time to time, to cry a bit for his own losses.

And after such a life of strength and beauty, love and redemption, sorrow and reconciliation, after such a life of performance and intimacy, leadership and tenderness, craftiness and craft, play and work, insecurity and swagger, he closes his eyes around death at Kaiser Hospital on Valentine's Day, the day of love, at the hour of the full moon, I and Richard holding his great and beautiful hands, telling him through our tears how much we love him.

The final chapter of life may need to be told for many people who have suffered through long or dreadful illnesses that have become major players in their lives. For a woman who lived for several years with a crippling disease, for example, you might talk about how this disease shaped her life, how she dealt with its degenerative effects, and how she used humor to live with it. For a man who waged his battles with cancer on several fronts and won many of them, you could mention some of what he told you about what he had learned from his dialogue with his body. Often I have observed that family relationships change as a result of an illness, and sometimes it is appropriate to speak of those changes in a context of gratitude for the epiphanies of love and grace that uplifted and nourished families through their last weeks, hours, and days together.

When someone has died of an illness that has called for a great deal of caregiving and patience on the part of family, family members may also have issues with regard to the roles they have had during this final chapter. The son who took care of Mom for the last three years may feel resentful toward the brother and sister who lived at a distance and made only occasional visits. The other brother and sister may feel guilty or isolated. It may be enough to name their feelings in general ways. Or one could mention the devotion of those who have cared for her and the gift of intimate relationship they received, while acknowledging gratitude for the precious moments others were able to have with her in spite of their physical separation.

A long illness in particular has become a way of life for others in a family. For example, a man who was a devoted caregiver may be at a loss to know what he will do with his life, which has been consumed with his role. Even if death is a welcome relief from suffering, he faces a time of adjustment. The woman who could not handle the role of caregiver may feel a sense of guilt. She loved her husband, but she is relieved, not only that his pain is over but also that she can go on with her life. Some words in the service, perhaps in a general statement in the prayer, can speak to issues of loss or guilt without intruding on anyone's privacy.

In short, it is helpful to make a space in the service for acknowledgment of the fact that an illness has affected those who gather to grieve.

As important as it is to provide space in our rituals for a broad range of feelings, be wary of using a memorial service or family ritual to address individual issues of guilt and anger. I attended a service on one occasion where one member of the family took it upon herself in a public gathering to tell other individuals in the family that her brother, who had spoken with her before he died, forgave them for their various offenses. The other members of the family were mortified that she would single them out and presume to speak on behalf of her brother. Her intent was to give them comfort and ease their pain. Instead, they became angry with her for choosing this inappropriate time to "air the family's dirty linen." It would have been more appropriate for her to meet with them in a private gathering to share what her brother had confided.

Death is the great equalizer, but all deaths are not equal. How a person dies will often shape aspects of the grieving process for those who have loved that individual. Whatever the circumstances, however, it is important to focus not on the way a person died but on the way he or she lived and to plan for rituals worthy of that life.

CHAPTER SEVEN

Family Ties and Family Lies

When Your Family Is Alienated

SEVERAL YEARS AGO, I SAW A CARTOON THAT DEPICTED A LARGE AUDITORIUM set up as though for a convention. The banner across the auditorium read, "Adult Children of Normal Parents," and below it, all alone in the rows and rows of seats, sat one solitary person.

Even the most loving and harmonious families have their imperfections. At no time are we more aware of our familial flaws than when a family member dies. I have worked with countless families who were estranged at the time of a death. I have also experienced estrangement among members of my own family and have a personal perspective on how important it is to find ways to acknowledge the grief that is wrapped up in the ongoing pain of alienation.

Ritual expression cannot heal or erase the wounds of a broken relationship, but it can help people face up to and identify the nature of their pain. There are some basic principles for calming the waters if family members are estranged:

- *Be sure that individuals who are not in the family are present.* Their presence creates a community context and provides for all family members to feel supported by those whom they have invited. A community context is also an invitation to call a timeout—a truce of sorts. The focus is not on personal estrangements but rather on the need to remember well.

- *The person leading the ceremony should not be identified with any side of the family.* This person may be one individual's spiritual guide or counselor but must be able to relate with and care for all members of the family.

- *Regardless of religious beliefs or lack of them, the setting for the ceremony or service must be acknowledged as sacred space.* The "turf" does not belong to anyone, even though some members in a family will be more involved in making decisions than others. Sacred space provides a place for each person in his or her own way to feel the presence of a larger dimension of reality. For a Christian, this may be the Holy Spirit; for a scientific deist, it may be cosmic stardust. The point is not necessarily to say what that larger dimension is but to provide a context for its presence to be felt.

- *Don't expect to satisfy everyone in attendance.* It is unlikely that any ceremony will serve the needs of all individuals who gather, whether they are estranged or not. Mourners who feel that a ceremony has not provided space for their particular pain should consider creating another ritual that will address their needs.

Since all families—and their conflicts as well as their joys—are different, it is nearly impossible to describe all the permutations of situations, let alone map out solutions to the problems that seep into a memorial service. The personal stories, rituals, and examples related in this chapter are intended to serve as inspiration for ways families can create meaningful memorial rituals in order to invite a spirit of healing into their midst.

THE WATERS OF HEALING

At sixteen, Stephanie had just had about the best summer ever. She had won a scholarship for gifted students to work and study underwater life alongside some of the world's foremost marine scientists. She knew her skills as an expert swimmer and deep-sea diver would serve her well in her choice to pursue a career in oceanography.

Before the summer ended, however, she and her younger brother, Ned, would have to journey to Indiana to visit with their father. It was part of the contractual agreement that had been forged when their parents divorced two years before. They loved their father—that wasn't it. But they knew they would be on their own most of the time, since he drank heavily through the night and slept most of the day.

He had promised them a ride in his new boat, so they hoped maybe this year would be different. It was different, for a while anyway, as they motored out into the lake and anchored near an island for a picnic. He had been drinking the whole time, however, and soon after they ate, he passed out. Stephanie and Ned swam and relaxed through the afternoon; then Ned fell asleep on the boat deck. At dusk, Stephanie tried to wake her father, but he did not respond. She then attempted to start the motor so they could get back to the marina before dark, but long weeds tangled and paralyzed the propeller. Comfortable with underwater activity, she dived in to clear the propeller.

At least that is what Ned later surmised. He woke up while she was in the water cleaning off the propeller and was concerned that it was getting dark. Unable to rouse his father and assuming that his sister was in the boat's cabin, he pressed the button to start the engine. In a few moments, he saw scraps of his sister's bathing suit churning to the top of the water. The father, who was completely blacked out, did not even hear Ned's cries for help.

One can only imagine the rage, pain, and guilt suffered by the members of this family. The minister in Stephanie's hometown wanted to incorporate some elements in the ritual that would make space for the depth of their pain. He knew he wanted ocean water for the ritual, because of Stephanie's love for the ocean, so he traveled three hours each way to collect a sample from the Atlantic Ocean. With help from some of Stephanie's friends, he filled little vials with the water so that everyone (especially teens) could have something to take from the service with them.

On the day of the service, the high school closed for the afternoon. After a powerful service that celebrated Stephanie's life and included the mournfully haunting recorded sounds of humpbacked whales, several hundred people, mostly high school students, processed to a lovely rural cemetery. Rain poured over the crowd huddled around Stephanie's gravesite. After offering a scripture reading and brief remarks, the minister turned off the microphone and addressed the family. He spoke of the healing and purifying qualities of water, as well as its universal connection to the eternal rhythms of life in many traditions. He spoke of Stephanie's love for the ocean and her passionate longing to explore its mysteries. He then touched the foreheads of Stephanie's father and brother and mother with the water. He was Christian, but he knew Stephanie had embraced earth-centered spirituality, so he then walked slowly around her casket and at each corner sprinkled some of the water into the wind and rain in the four directions.

The minister knew, of course, that his cleansing ritual would not "wash away" the guilt and rage that filled so many hearts that day, but his gesture invited a spiritual power of healing into their midst in a way that his spoken prayers could not. Likewise the drops of water that people took away with them signaled a continued need for the power to be at work in their lives. Perhaps they would find a way to use it at a later time. Even the funeral director, who had not known Stephanie, took a vial of water, a tangible token of the power he had felt at work in the ceremony.

In addition, this minister had invited each member of Stephanie's family to write a note that would be buried in the casket with Stephanie's body. This was their opportunity to offer a private message in the context of a public ceremony.

It was painful for Stephanie's mother to be in the presence of her estranged husband, the man whose drunken stupor had contributed to her daughter's death and her son's anguish. The ritual honored her rage at the same time that it held it in the context of a larger realm of divine grace. Stephanie's father carried a burden of guilt that others, in their anger and grief, could not hold in their care. The ritual of writing the letter gave him a context for private confession. Stephanie's brother, whose memory of pressing the button to start the motor would haunt him for his entire life, was held in the care of loving community. The minister's gesture of blessing offered an unspoken acknowledgment of the burdens carried by each member of Stephanie's family. Witnessed by a throng of people who created a circle of compassion, the ritual helped begin a long, long process of letting go. How fitting that it was punctuated with a bagpiper's rendering of "Amazing Grace."

FAMILY SECRETS

Family secrets carry an amazing power to create and maintain unhealthy divisions and alliances within families. According to rabbi and psychologist Edwin H. Friedman, family secrets fall into four categories.

First, there is the kind where one member gives information to another member and asks him or her not to tell the rest of the family. For example, a son gets arrested and tells his mother and asks her not to tell Dad. Or a daughter realizes she is a lesbian and tells her sister but does not want their parents to know.

The second kind is where the family, without conscious efforts, has conspired to keep information closeted. Perhaps Grandma committed suicide, but no one talks about it. Or Dad served a little time in prison many years ago. Suicide, crime, alcoholism, child abuse, incest, and mental illness are some of the most common family secrets.

The third kind is more subtle. An example is when Dad tells Daughter how upset Mother was when she found out Daughter was getting married. Daughter never checks that out with Mother. Or perhaps Mother and Father have divorced and talk about each other to the children, but the children do not say anything.

The fourth kind of family secret is the unmentionable subject—something no one can talk about, like the death of Mother's first child at age six, twenty years ago.

Whatever brand of family secret is at play, the effects are the same. Honest communication is compromised; alliances dependent on being in or out of "the know" are falsely intimate. Sometimes people will keep secrets to protect others from being hurt, but their dishonesty creates barriers, and the secrets are more hurtful concealed than they would be revealed. A family secret needs to be revealed with sensitivity, however, and with the potential for changing some of the dynamics of relationship that perpetuated the secret. Timing is important, too.

For Charles and Jeannette, whose father died when they were both in their forties, poor timing aggravated the pain of their loss.

Their father, Jim, died at the age of eighty. Maude, Jim's wife (their stepmother), was in charge of the service. Since Jim was irreverently nonreligious, others in the family were surprised when Maude chose to plan the service in the Mormon tradition of her upbringing. But she also took some care to invite participation from them.

Maude and Jim had been married for eighteen years, having wed shortly after Jim and Betty (Charles and Jeannette's mother) were divorced. Jim's children always enjoyed visiting with him and Maude, except for worrying about getting crumbs on Maude's immaculate carpet or leaving a sign of human presence in her shiny bathroom sink. Jim and Maude were fun to be with, and it was obvious that they were very much in love with each other. Betty also happily remarried after her divorce from Jim. Charles and Jeannette did not really know what events had ended their parents' thirty-two year marriage, but they accepted that the estranged couple preferred not to be at any family gathering together.

Charles and Jeannette mourned their father's death. A Kansas native who grew up with Midwestern values, Jim was kind and generous. His friends knew he would "give them the shirt off his back," and his business associates could count on him to be ethical in all dealings. He taught his children to be honest above all things.

Jim was also a family man. The trouble was that he had two families. Charles and Jeannette found out about the other family sometime between their father's death and his funeral. That is when Maude decided it was time to tell the truth about her long affair with Jim.

Her timing could not have been worse. Shedding the burden of her long-held secret, she told Charles and Jeannette that she and Jim had been lovers since before Charles was born. This news, delivered the day before the funeral, stirred memories for Charles especially of his father's absence throughout his childhood—weekends and holidays when he was "working" out of town. Maude told them what a wonderful father Jim had been to her son, Frank. For example, Jim had bought Frank a shiny new bike one year for Christmas. She was not aware, as she told Charles this story, that Charles had received a used bicycle because the family could not afford a new one.

There was no way for Maude's Mormon pastor to accommodate the anger Charles and Jeannette felt, not only toward Maude but also toward their father. They went through the motions of the ritual and affirmed the qualities they loved about Jim. The good things people said were all true. But Charles and Jeannette carried the fresh wound of their father's betrayal.

Charles's wife spoke during the service. She made no reference to Jim's double life. For Charles and Jeannette, however, this person who knew what they knew was able to carry some of their feelings into sacred space and affirm the love Jim had for them in spite of his "limitations" as a father.

Another issue exacerbated Charles and Jeanette's pain, however. Upon their father's death, Maude inherited all of his estate.

What happens to an estate is a common source of alienation between children and their parents or stepparents at the time of a death. Many divisions result from an unhappy allocation of money or property. After eighteen years of marriage, Maude surely deserved to inherit a large portion of what she and Jim had accumulated. But it was also her responsibility to assure his children that a portion of their father's estate would eventually come to them. Instead, her son claimed the entire estate when he arranged for Maude to live in a retirement home.

Money and possessions take on new meaning when a death occurs. Their power to offer affirmation or negation of love has no equal. For example, a woman named Anita was a teenager when her mother died. Anita also had a younger sister. A year after her mother's death, her father married a widow who had three children. The Brady Bunch they were not, but Anita was fond of her stepmother and the "little sisters" with whom she shared a home and family for several years. So it was particularly painful for her when, after her father's death, her stepmother chose to keep everything that had belonged to her birth mother—family heirlooms, some of her mother's jewelry, and the good dishes that came out on holidays. When Anita appealed to her stepmother to give her some of her mother's belongings—things that she "grew up with"—she received some of the less valuable jewelry.

The more subtle pain for Anita was her father's failure to provide for her in his will. Even a statement that clearly left some of her mother's family heirlooms to her would have made a tremendous difference.

By the time they attended the memorial service for Anita's father, the tension between Anita and her stepmother was palpable. Anita was fortunate to have some close friends with whom she could share her sense of compounded loss. Although they had not known her father, they attended the service, sitting immediately behind Anita so she could sense their support.

How parents decide on the distribution of their possessions sometimes provides a barometer of relationships. Dad gets in the last word when the son who disappointed him is cut out of the will. Mother nurses her anger at one daughter by leaving her prized antiques to the other daughter. Old wounds are reopened or new ones are inflicted in postmortem assaults.

For those of you who may find yourselves planning to communicate your anger or resentment through distribution of your estate, please consider that your own spirit will benefit from exploring other more honest or direct ways to convey your anger or displeasure. You may have good reasons for wanting to distribute your possessions in a manner that favors some members of your family over others (or bypasses them all in favor of a worthy cause), but you need to let them know your reasons when you write the will so that you will not leave them to draw their own conclusions after you die.

Those who feel attacked by gestures of revenge, resentment, or greed need to be aware that these vindictive gestures are desperate cries from the spiritually bereft. The power that a person did not have in life translates into a manipulative grasp from the grave. If you are on the receiving end of this last sad gasp, it may help you to be able to recognize that the attack comes from a place not of power but of powerlessness. It is more about the other person than about you.

Grief is a positive process. But there is a kind of dynamic that can develop, particularly when you are alienated from the person who died, that is destructive. It occurs when you need your anger to shield you from some of the deeper issues of your grief. Just as surely as you can numb or avoid your pain with tranquilizers or alcohol, so too you can stay angry and avoid dealing with the sources of deeper pain in the relationship. The real loss is never the inheritance. The real loss is the relationship that failed. The deepest and most difficult grieving we do is about what is unresolved in our relationships. Anger may be a starting place, but if you do not get past it to the fear or deeper loss, there is no healthy resolution.

Anger, however, is what you feel when you have just gotten that slap on your tear-streaked face. Anger and hurt. If you are creating a memorial service to honor the person who has just given the knife in your belly a last twist, you have to find private ways to express your anger while you plan for a more public ceremony. This is not a denial of a very legitimate feeling; it is a realistic recognition of what you need to do.

Although my mother did not exclude me from her will, I discovered, when she died, that she had given her valuable jewelry and some lovely china dishes to the woman who cleaned her house. She was angry because I had moved away to pursue training for the ministry and was not physically present to help the family through my younger brother's serious illness. I did not particularly care about the jewelry, but I felt the indirect message in her having given away what would have been mine. The dishes were tangible reminders of a happy childhood; I wanted them.

I spent the morning alone in her room, sobbing through anger and pain. This catharsis helped. I also allowed myself to feel the pain of having let her down. I did not regret my career decisions, but I still felt sad that I had disappointed her. Then I wrote a letter to her that I would read at her committal ceremony. Actually I wrote several letters until I had one that could contain the pain and anger without being overtaken by it. "Dear Mother," began my missive, which assumed a poetic style as I wrote:

You have chiseled your spirit into my soul:
—sometimes it sustains
—sometimes it hurts deeply.
Yet I know of no one else who could so perfectly carve dark secret long-
ings into tree limbs—who could so perfectly shape pain into beauty.
You were an easy person to love. That simple truth was always in your
grasp, but you wanted it too much to receive it.
You knew your demons and your angels.
You laughed fully and cried soulfully.
You loved what you hated and you hated what you loved.
You embraced life at its roots while you cursed its cruel and merciless
strokes of injustice.
You were Gretchen. You were Mother.
You were a woman, and,
Take you for all and all, we shall not look upon your like again.
We plant you here where azalea and narcissus will awaken to greet you
each spring
Where water will trickle through earth veins
Where wild vines rise up and choke away the weaker growth
Where shadow creek meets the sun
And death and life are One.
Earth to earth . . . ashes to ashes . . . dust to dust.

I read the letter because our ceremony was small and private. The family
and friends present understood the complexities of this wonderful but self-
destructive woman. Had it been more public, I might have asked a few others to join me in a separate ritual where I would read it aloud. The point I wish

to make is this: My cathartic sobbing helped. Writing the letter helped. Reading the letter aloud in the presence of others also helped. Somehow this part of my ritual provided space for me to be hurt without having my pain intrude on my expressing the deep and abiding love and gratitude I felt for my mother.

A HIERARCHY OF GRIEF?

Whatever flaws we have in our imperfect families, we will be aware of them at a memorial ritual. Those who are in charge of the planning may not even be aware of ways that they aggravate tensions or create new ones. For example, a man's children put together a collage of photographs for display at his service. Their selection of pictures did not include any photos of him with their stepmother, whom he had married only a year before he died. It was not that they intended to exclude her. They just gathered photos from their own collections, which did not contain any pictures of her. It did not occur to them in the midst of their own grief to ask her for contributions.

Sometimes stepparents or former spouses are discounted in rites of passage, and it is often not an intentional affront. When my stepson died, for example, dozens of cards and letters came addressed to my husband only. I had known and loved Tom for twenty-seven of his twenty-eight years, but I was not included in messages from many people who were my friends or were members of my congregation. Similarly, people are awkward about how to include the former spouse of someone who has died. A former spouse will grieve differently from a current one, but will grieve nonetheless. If there are children from that relationship, the former spouse will grieve also on their behalf.

One of the most common ways to slight a stepparent or a former spouse is to give them no designated seating at a formal gathering. Just as family receive reserved seating areas in a wedding, so too with a death ritual. What is the unspoken message at a wedding, for example, when a mother is escorted into the gathering and a stepmother is not? It is the same message she receives at a funeral when she is left out of the family reception or left to find transportation while others take their seats in black limousines.

Another commonly excluded or offended person is the surviving partner in a committed gay or lesbian relationship. This will frequently be apparent in death notices written up by newspaper staff. When Jane Chambers died, for example, her obituary was published in the *New York Times*. Although she and Beth Allen had been a couple for fourteen years, the obituary read, "She leaves her mother, Clarice, of Florida, and two brothers, Henry and Ben." Beth was mentioned earlier as a "long-time companion" who shared a home with Jane. The truth is that for most of Jane's adult life, the people she considered family were not blood relations.

It is up to those planning a ritual to think in terms of inclusion. It is helpful, particularly when family members are alienated, to have a facilitator for the service who can care for the inclusion of each person. If there is a dynamic of alienation, for example, between a parent who meets to plan the service and a child or stepchild who lives at a distance, the service leader can make a long-distance call. Included in this way, the distanced family members feel more a part of the planning. Also, the service leader, aware of their perspective, can find ways to represent it in remarks or prayers.

WHO OWNS THE BODY?

A sensitive issue sometimes comes up around the decisions that are made with regard to the body of the person who has died. If there is a husband or wife, that person will usually have the authority to make the decision. If the couple was not legally married (as is the case for almost all same-sex couples), the surviving partner's rights may be in question. (Estranged parents of a gay or lesbian person may dispute the rights of the partner, unless those rights are clear in the laws of the state where the person died.) If a child has died, the parents decide. If there is a custodial parent in an estranged marriage, that parent's wishes will carry more weight.

If whoever is vested with this responsibility is either alienated from or insensitive to others in the family, it is a source of additional grief for those who are not included in the decisions. This is particularly true when cremation has been chosen and one member or segment of a family keeps the ashes rather than burying or scattering them. It is also the case when someone takes the ashes and conducts a solitary ceremony.

Closure happens best when you commit the remains of a body somewhere final. Dust to dust, not dust to living room table or bedroom nightstand. You may need to delay committal for a time, but eventually you need to release what belongs to creation. You do not own a person's cremated remains. To keep them or to distribute them privately is to deprive other family members of an opportunity for their closure. It sets you apart in a way that may very well offend the spirit of the person whose remains you clutch to yourself.

That said, for those who have kept a container of ashes for over a year, think of what it is you need to keep, really, as a remembrance of the person whose death you still mourn. Consider gathering some mementos and photographs that you can place in a special memorial location. Or perhaps think about creating a memorial site outdoors. There are many options. Then, on the anniversary of the person's death, his or her birthday, or some other significant date, invite others who still grieve to join you for a brief committal ceremony (options are discussed in Chapter Eight). Send them a copy of this book or contact a minister in your religious tradition and begin your planning together. The ritual will give you an opportunity to remember well, to grieve, and to create a community of caring with others.

IRRECONCILABLE ESTRANGEMENT

Many readers of this book may be so alienated from someone in their families that they are entirely cut off. They have not spoken to one another for years. Perhaps they are wounded by sexual abuse, violent aggression, unforgivable betrayals, or deep misunderstandings.

Unfortunately and understandably, the human impulse under these circumstances is to avoid the memorial ritual altogether. In some cases, the process of mourning a broken relationship has gone on for a long time. Many people have to let go of hopes for reconciliation in order to live a productive life.

There is no simple advice for those of you who will experience a death under these circumstances, except to say that you need to participate in a ritual of closure. If you can attend a funeral or memorial, even one that does not speak to you in terms of your spiritual or emotional needs, go. It will be painful, but if you do not grieve, the pain you avoid at the time of death will haunt you in years to come. What you need is a safe context for feeling and expressing your pain. If you attend, be sure you have at least one person with you whose role is to support you. If you are traveling away from home, take special care of yourself. Be sure you are comfortable with where you will stay. Know your own limits in terms of the time you will spend with the people with whom you are in tension. Know where you are going to sit. Will you be with other family members? Separate? Also, you should know ahead of time what you need and can realistically expect from going. Although there may be opportunities for reconciliation, that should not be your expectation or goal.

If you cannot attend, or if you want to hold a more personally crafted memorial in addition to one that others have created, you may want to work with a counselor or clergy or wise friend who can help you shape a ceremony that meets your particular needs. The guidelines for a personal ritual draw from the same principles set forth at the beginning of this chapter:

- Provide a context of community. Be sure to have at least one person as a witness.

- Prepare sacred space. In whatever location you choose for a ritual, make the space sacred, appealing to your senses. You may want music or flowers or herbs or incense. Objects such as photographs, mementos, flowers, rocks, or religious symbols may help you evoke memory in a sacred context. Or you might just place a lovely cloth on a small table and use a single candle. Above all, the space needs to feel safe.

- Designate sacred time. Give yourself the gift of a time set aside for the ritual. It should be at least two hours.

- Declare your intent. What do you want to accomplish in a ritual? What feelings do you want to have held in the space? Which of your needs can (and cannot) be met?

- Using guidelines or ideas provided in this book, plan a memorial ceremony that will address your specific needs. Because this is a personal and more private ritual, you have the opportunity to express and address your own emotional needs in a safe environment.

- When the ceremony is over, share a meal, go out for coffee, take a walk, or in some way celebrate the gift of ritual expression that you have just given yourself.

A TIME OUT OF TIME

There is one last important point to keep in mind when you are planning for memorial rituals when there are family tensions or wounds from the past. At the time of a death, you enter a space and time that are out of the ordinary. Whether or not you recognize this as sacred, think of it as holding potential that does not exist in ordinary time. With the death of a relative, something has died in you, too. You are reminded of the failures as well as the gifts of relationship. You are more aware that you live in a fragile human body. While you are in this extra-ordinary time, you have a heightened consciousness of what is precious, what is true. This is the case not only for you but also for others in your family. There is potential for connecting, truth telling, and reconciling. Even if you are not alienated, you may find yourself realizing that you want to have more quality in your relationships. Extra-ordinary time is a time apart, when you and those you call family gather not only to remember the person who died but also to remember the bonds of kinship between and among you.

CHAPTER EIGHT

Earth, Air, Fire, Water

Committal Ceremonies

When Barbara and Harry went on their first date, Harry produced a bottle of champagne and two glasses from the glove compartment. So when Harry died twenty years later, there had to be champagne. And a bagpipe. And balloons.

"I didn't want the memorial service to be a downer for the children," said Barbara, speaking of Harry's grandchildren.

Of course there were tears, but the upbeat service was primarily a celebration of Harry's life. Family and friends gathered in the seaside home where Barbara and Harry had spent many vacations. They shared memories, drank champagne, and ate cheese and sausage. The sound of the bagpiper coming up the street summoned them outdoors, where every person received five helium-filled balloons tethered to a string. Each balloon contained a small amount of Harry's cremated remains (enough to be symbolic without flouting legal restrictions).

Barbara took her place in the center of a circle, then let go of her string, signaling all to follow suit.

This was an unusual committal ceremony, but it was devised in response to Harry's life. The physical release of the colorful balloons was Barbara's symbol of letting go of Harry's body in a manner that was in keeping with his spirit.

Committal is the inclusive term used to describe the burial or distribution of a person's bodily remains. A committal ceremony may be the only ceremony conducted (as for example, a graveside service). More often it will precede or follow a memorial service or will be part of a traditional funeral. In recent years, however, there has been a trend toward separating the two. People who elect cremation often delay both the memorial and the committal ceremony to allow time to gather family and plan a meaningful service. Those who choose to bury the body may also want more time to plan a memorial. So they will hold the burial ceremony shortly after death and schedule the memorial for a few weeks to a month later. Also, separating the two gives people the option of having a public memorial service and a private committal ceremony.

The common theme for all committal ceremonies, regardless of what alternative has been chosen for the body, is the return to creation and to the giver or source of life. Perhaps intuitively, perhaps because tradition draws from these archetypal images, families will opt to employ one or more of the four basic elements in their ritual: earth, air, fire and water. Barbara gravitated toward the lighter, uplifting qualities of air, wind, and sky in her ritual with the balloons because she wanted to "celebrate" Harry. Many people choose to scatter cremated remains on water, where the ashes are blended with a flowing, living force of creation. Fire, its smoke rising on the wind, is incorporated in the ritual of cremation and in other rituals of blessing and letting go that may be included in committal ceremonies. Burial in the earth continues to be the most universal rite of closure. In a site aboveground in a mausoleum, both earth and air elements are called forth.

Any committal ceremony that does not take place in a legally designated burial site such as a cemetery must be conducted according to state or provincial laws. A state-by-state discussion of resources and restrictions is included in *Caring for the Dead: Your Final Act of Love* by Lisa Carlson (see Recommended Reading and Resources at the back of the book).

The following discussions describe some of the ways families have identified with the elements of earth, air, fire, and water and have used them in personalized rituals of committal.

EARTH

"Remember thou art dust, and to dust thou shalt return." These lines from the biblical book of Genesis speak to the human understanding of death as a return to the earth from whence we have come. Burial of a person's body or ashes in the ground often includes burial of significant objects. In the service for Ruth Codier, described in Chapter One, Ruth's family filled a clay vessel with earth from Ruth's birthplace, along with a stone and other personally meaningful items. They broke the vessel over Ruth's ashes. This moving ritual evoked images of the eternal in the temporal, the beginning in the end—the natural rhythms of life of which we are a part.

What people choose to bury with someone's body or ashes is a very individual matter. Sometimes it may be something that just needs to stay with the person—a child's teddy bear, a teen's favorite CD, Dad's old golf shoes, a handmade valentine that Grandma cherished.

Stones, ancient and archetypal, are often used for burial rites. The primitive custom of piling rocks in a location to create a cairn provides a variety of possibilities for participation. (Cairns can also be created in any location to mark a memorial site.) In an ancient Israeli custom, for example, people are invited to place a stone on a covered grave as they leave and ask forgiveness for any injustice they may have committed against the person who has died.

Another ancient burial rite is the scattering or tossing of flowers into a grave. William Shakespeare's description of the burial of Ophelia in the tragedy *Hamlet* comes to mind. Ophelia, who had gone "mad" after her father's death, drowned with flowers garlanded over her body. Shortly before she was found in the river, she had spoken to the king and queen of Denmark in the language of flowers, offering rosemary for remembrance and pansies for thoughts. She offered columbine (for folly) and fennel (for flattery), but she said she could not find violets (for faithfulness), for they "withered all" when her father died. At her grave, Hamlet's mother, the queen, tossed flowers into the earth, saying:

Sweets to the sweet! Farewell.
I hoped thou shouldst have been my Hamlet's wife.
I thought thy bride bed to have decked, sweet maid,
And not have strewed thy grave.

The ancient language of flowers is spoken at many a committal ceremony. Ophelia drew from traditional British imagery in her offering of rosemary for remembrance, and every flower in the queen's bouquet bespoke a message. Although more and more people choose to invite friends to make donations to worthy causes "in lieu of flowers," there is still a place for using the language of flowers—for invoking their symbolism and inviting people to choose flowers that speak for them. Rosemary, a wonderfully fragrant common herb, is easily grown or available in grocery stores. It is suitable for almost any committal ceremony.

Rosemary is for remembrance. Here are some additional flowers and herbs that might be tossed into a grave, planted over a grave, or given to people to take with them, along with their traditional associated meaning:

Bellflower *Gratitude*
Bluebell *Constancy*
Camellia (white) *Perfected loveliness*
Carnation *"Alas my poor heart!"*
Chervil *Sincerity*
China rose *Beauty always new*
Chrysanthemum (red) *"I love"*
Daffodil *Regard*
Dogwood *Durability*
Forget-me-not *True love*
Geranium (red) *Comforting*
Gladiolus *Strong character*
Gloxinia *Proud spirit*
Heliotrope *Devotion*
Hollyhock *Ambition*
Honeysuckle *Devoted affection*
Hyacinth *Sport, game, play*
Ivy *Fidelity*
Jasmine (white) *Amiability*
Jasmine (yellow) *Grace, elegance*
Larkspur *Lightness, levity*

Lilac (purple) *Love's first emotions*
Lilac (white) *Youthful innocence*
Lily (white) *Purity, sweetness*
Lily-of-the-valley *Return of happiness*
Magnolia *Love of nature*
Marigold *Grief*
Mint *Virtue*
Morning glory *Affection*
Nasturtium *Patriotism*
Pansy *"Thinking of you"*
Primrose *Early youth*
Rose *Love*
Rosebud (red) *Purity and loveliness*
Roses (red and white) *Unity*
Sage *Esteem*
Salvia (blue) *"I think of you"*
Salvia (red) *"Forever yours"*
Scilla (blue) *Forgiveness*
Sunflower (dwarf) *Adoration*

Sweet pea *Delicate pleasures*	Woodbine *Fraternal love*
Sweet William *Gallantry*	Zinnia *Thoughts of an absent*
Tulip (red) *Declaration of love*	*friend*

Of course, there is nothing wrong with choosing flowers because they are a person's favorites or because of your own positive associations with them.

AIR

Air is wind, sky, and sun. It is also breath, which translates, in some languages, as "spirit." Air gives life, uplifts, lightens. Rituals that incorporate images of air call forth its nourishment, its mystery, and its inspiration. People who want to emphasize a spirit of triumph or celebration in their ritual will sometimes choose images of hope borne on air and extending into unlimited space.

Planting a tree, flower, or bulb over an earthen grave is a gesture of faith and hope. Life springs from death as roots take hold in centuries of compost and a plant reaches for the light. Launching a balloon or balloons also affirms a resurrection of sorts—a journey from this world into the next. (There is some debate about the environmental impact of certain kinds of balloons; Mylar is unquestionably a hazard.)

Sound, too, travels on air. In a church in New England, every memorial service ends with the ringing of the church bell, which has a rope that each person can pull when leaving the sanctuary. The ringing of the bell offers a song of life and memory into the air. An adaptation of this ritual for a committal ceremony might be the use of chimes or another wind-powered instrument. The popularity of the bagpipe may be as much for its airborne echoes and breathy timbre as for its traditional symbolism.

Scent, which travels on air, is powerfully evocative—so much so that it is advisable to be aware of why you are using a particular scent. What is it that you wish to evoke in your choice? Is there a comfort for you in using incense, for example, that is associated with a religious tradition? Does the scent encourage relaxation or healing? Do you associate it with the person who has died? Also, you may want to consider the negative side of using scent. Will people present have to deal with allergic reactions from either the scent or smoke? (I recall doing a "smudging" ceremony with sage once, and one person present had a severe allergic reaction and had to leave the room. I regretted that my ritual inadvertently excluded him.)

A creative approach to the theme of air and transformation is a ritual of freeing butterflies. You can purchase a tube of cocoons at a science store (there is usually a store of this type in large shopping malls) and schedule the committal ceremony for the time when the package directions indicate that the butterflies will emerge. As the body or the ashes are being committed, you open the container, and the butterflies fly away.

There is no limit to the ways people express their airborne sentiments. The family of a young man who died suddenly wanted to launch their blessings to him into space at the time of his burial. This they did with a small homemade rocket, with children taking an active role filling the rocket with small mementos and notes. They continue to launch their messages into space on each anniversary of the man's death.

Although you may wish to avoid rituals with negative environmental implications or with the logistical preparations involved in launching balloons or butterflies, these gestures can be very powerful and uplifting, particularly when they accompany a spoken affirmation of the continuity of life.

FIRE

Fire purifies, and its smoke is lifted on air into the mystery of unending space. Fire is light in the darkness and warmth from the cold. It is the traditional focus for the home, where women, in particular, have attended to the hearth.

Fire was a theme for Lucia's unusual committal service—a ritual she designed herself. Lucia could name every tree, shrub, flower, and herb in her surroundings, and those who attended her service gathered in her backyard, where they formed a circle around an open-pit fire. Branches of evergreen and serviceberry wreathed the fire. Each person there was invited to throw a branch into the flames and offer a blessing for Lucia. (There is a belief in some cultures that blessings rise in the smoke.) Some of Lucia's ashes were scattered in her yard among the plants and trees she loved. Not all of her remains were committed at the ceremony proper, however. In a ritual of community, Lucia's daughter had prepared sachets from garden herbs and Lucia's ashes. These she gave to the people who gathered and asked them to scatter or place the ashes in a location that was beautiful or special to them.

WATER

Water is life, always changing, always the same. Like fire, it purifies. It also refreshes and heals. In its many forms, it is one form, and from its many sources, there is one source. In its simplicity and complexity, water is a universal symbol of the life from which we came and to which we shall return. To blend one's remains with water is to surrender the spirit back to the giver of life and claim one's timeless place in creation. Many individuals who ask to have their ashes committed in water do so because this gesture affirms their attraction to water and their sense of connection with the rhythms of the natural world.

For Celia, committal at sea meant that she was going home. Celia died in her late thirties after a six-month struggle with cancer. In a very brief and simple ceremony at sea, Celia's husband, mother, and two children chartered a boat and went to the legally required boundary, which was three miles out to sea. They turned the motor off and allowed the boat to drift quietly while they took in the vast and silent waters all around them. Her husband, Joe, held the cardboard container of ashes, on which the children had drawn or pasted pictures and messages of love to their mother. Then Joe spoke:

> Celia loved the ocean—the feel of the wind on her face, the thrill of riding a wave, the peace of walking along the tide line with a friend, the sweet comfort of sitting on the beach watching Kim and Laura make sand castles. She loved sunrises and sunsets, the smell of salt air and the sound of the surf. She was at home in the water, not just as a swimmer but as a child of the Spirit rocked in its billowing swells even while fearful of its mysterious depths. This is where she wanted us to bring her ashes. She makes friends now with the shadows below. She joins the spirits of her father, her grandparents, and our first child, who died before we could welcome him into our world. We commit her ashes now to the sea and beyond, where she may be blessed in peace eternal.
>
> Earth to earth, ashes to ashes, dust to dust.

In tearful silence, Joe opened the box and handed it to Celia's mother. She carefully checked the direction of the wind, opened the sealed plastic bag, and poured the ashes over the side of the boat. Kim and Laura then picked up a basket of rose petals that they had prepared earlier and scattered the petals on the water. Joe tossed a single long-stemmed red rose after the petals.

Joe and his family had planned for this simple ceremony in advance. He was prone to seasickness, so he took a medication and kept the ceremony short so they would not be rocking on the water an undue amount of time.

A postscript to this story is that Joe and the children kept the container that the children had decorated. A large jar was placed inside it, and for the first year after Celia's death, the family placed fresh flowers in the jar for every holiday, birthday, or special occasion, as a gesture of loving remembrance. After the first year, they kept it for anniversary observances, sometimes adding more messages or pictures to the design. Eventually it became rather tattered and water-stained, and they decided that it had served its purpose. (Joe had also remarried and felt that it was time to retire the box.) On the fifth anniversary of Celia's death, they took photos of the box for the scrapbook they had made for Celia's public memorial service, then burned the box in the fireplace, affirming that their love was with her always just as her love was still with them. This was not an easy ritual for them to perform, but it gave them a sense of release that allowed Joe in particular to move into another relationship. It was most difficult for the children, for whom Celia's choice of committal at sea left no place where they could visit with her. The box had given them a tangible memorial.

There are numerous options for containers used for committal services, from the most elegant caskets to the humblest little box of ashes. A great deal has been written, including books and articles by consumer advocates who warn against getting ripped off by people in the funeral business who want to sell expensive containers. Simplicity and modesty are probably most to be recommended, more for spiritual reasons than for the sake of economy. A cardboard box decorated by children has more meaning than the costliest urn. A pine or cedar casket constructed by friends and neighbors speaks of love in every board and nail. Many people place cremated ashes in familiar household containers. One man used a cookie jar, commenting that his wife loved the jar and would have approved of the whimsical touch.

ANNIVERSARY COMMITTAL

When families choose cremation and delay the committal of the ashes, they have the option of choosing a time for the committal that suits their needs. If they have not held a committal ceremony within the first year after death, the anniversary presents an opportunity for doing so. The following ritual was crafted for such an occasion.

Sheldon had died in March after a brief illness. A memorial service was held shortly after his death, but his wife had kept his ashes in an urn for the year. After making sure it was legal in their state, the family decided to bury his ashes in their yard and plant a tree over them. Just deciding what kind of tree to plant gave them opportunities to think about what kind of leaf or fruit would best evoke memories of Sheldon. They finally settled on an apple tree, for its blossoms and its fruit, which Sheldon loved best in apple pie.

Before the ceremony, Sheldon's two adult sons dug the hole and purchased the tree and had a small plaque engraved. They had also gathered water from a river where Sheldon loved to fish. They invited a few friends to come for the ceremony, which would be followed by a potluck lunch.

Everyone met in the house first. The service leader greeted people there and told them the ritual would begin with a silent procession to the site the family had selected. The procession itself declared their intent and created sacred time and space. Sheldon's wife led the way, carrying the container of ashes. The service leader opened the ceremony, saying:

We come here on this brisk morning to remember Sheldon—to honor and bless his life, to commit his ashes to the earth, and to dedicate this apple tree to his memory.

Sheldon died a year ago. It has been a year of moving through the seasons of grief—a year of birthdays, anniversaries, holidays; a year of simple ordinary days when his gifts were remembered and his presence was deeply missed.

We ride through the seasons of grief as on the waves of the ocean. Sometimes grief takes us through the depths of pain as into a churning sea where we are drawn down into the dark and released into energy and light. Sometimes it catches us off guard, like a wave that hits from behind, and we have to struggle to get back into a life-giving current.

But through the seasons of grief, there is healing, and through healing, memory nourishes us. So it is we are here today. Sheldon offered many gifts in this world, and we still enjoy them. His life still sends ripples far and wide beyond our knowing. In this final rite, we affirm the ties that are not broken by death.

Sheldon's younger son read a poem he had written. Then Sheldon's wife opened the container of ashes and said, "Earth to earth, ashes to ashes, dust to dust." She poured some of the ashes into the hole. She handed the container to her sons, and they poured the rest. The two sons then placed the tree in the hole, and one of them offered some remarks about why they had chosen an apple tree. With respect for the sacred quality of the ritual, he added a light touch with some affectionate remarks about how Sheldon would be "on their case to harvest those apples before the birds got 'em or they all rotted on the ground." Each of them put a shovelful of dirt into the hole and then passed the shovel to their mother. She put it down and picked up a handful of dirt and passed the shovel on to the next person. When the hole was filled, the older son picked up the large can of river water and spoke about how Sheldon loved to fish in Gurney Creek, where they had gotten the water. He and his brother poured the water around the tree. Sheldon's wife read the words on the plaque, which was attached to a metal stake, and placed it in the ground near the tree.

The older son invited everyone to join in a litany of memory. (As you may recall from Chapter Two, the litany names occasions through the year when the dead are remembered, and each line is followed with the refrain, "We remember you.") Before the closing lines were read, people added their own lines, saying things like "When I need some advice about how to build something" or "When I eat a piece of apple pie." After each line. they all repeated the refrain from the litany: "We remember you."

The service leader closed with a prayer and invited everyone to enjoy a potluck lunch, which included, of course, apple juice and apple pie.

Sheldon's family chose to bury his ashes in the yard, where he had spent many hours trimming bushes and flipping hamburgers. Using private property for scattering or burial of ashes gives you options you may not have in a cemetery or public setting, but there are some issues you should consider before you do so. The most obvious is that private property usually gets sold out of the family, and the new owners will not have the same regard for the sacred burial site that you do. Unless you can protect the site legally in your written contracts, it is wise to select a site that is unlikely to be disturbed. Even so, there are no guarantees. Whether or not you bury ashes that remain in a container also becomes an issue. You need to allow your imagination to envision the worst desecration before burying a container of cremated remains on private property. You may have the option of protecting a site by establishing a family burial ground. If you are interested in exploring this possibility, the first thing to do is investigate the relevant state, provincial, or national laws.

THE WHEEL TURNS OVER: A SAMPLE COMMITTAL CEREMONY

Earth, air, fire, and water—each of these signals a return to creation, a transformation of life, a unity with the cosmic heartbeat. For those who resound to the poetry of the earth's rhythms and its chemistry of transformation, the following ceremony, conducted by Mark Belletini, a Unitarian Universalist minister, may speak to your heart as it does to mine. This service can be adapted for a committal on land or water. If there is a separate memorial service where people share their "memories of the gift received," this section can be deleted or replaced with another reading.

Opening
We are here to return the elements
that made up the body of _____ to the earth,
earth, air, fire, and water,
joined by the ligaments of the spirit,
the bindings of life and love.

> Let silence be our memorial garment today,
> the bright *(or hidden)* sun our scripture text,
> the breeze *(and/or birds)* our comforting choral anthem.

Blessed be this moment of transition and letting go.
Blessed be this sacred act.
Blessed is the mystery of life and death which is our own.

Sharing Memories

Next, during a period of silence, individuals may name the gifts the deceased bequeathed them that they find alive in their present lives and recall the person's ways of looking at the world, gestures, phrases, metaphors, humor, approaches, and so on. This time ends with the words "Let us proceed in peace and yield to the earth what we must yield."

Prayer

Love—as _____ reminded us all
and as ancient scripture testifies—
You are stronger than death.
You flow in our tears and in our embraces,
you flow in our memorial heartbeats
and hopeful vulnerability to all that is to come.
You enfold us on suddenly lonely nights with strong arms of thanksgiving
for every day we knew _____.
You trust us to learn to live without final answers.
You set us free every time we turn to face letting go, loss, and sorrow.
You reveal yourself every time we turn to another with respect, tenderness, reliability, and care.
Death has none of your brightness or beauty.
And so thus we bless you, Love, that you are with us in our troubles,
and in our transition. Praise!

Committal

ALL TOUCH THE CONTAINER WITH THEIR HANDS IN BLESSING AND SAY:

Ashes to ashes,
dust to dust,
memory to memory,
story to story,
blessing to blessing,
strength to strength,
gratitude to gratitude,
spirit to spirit,
love to love.
The wheel turns ever,
and what came out of the earth
returns to it now in peace.
The wheel turns ever,
yet whatsoever love and grace and gift
we know from _____ is at the center of that wheel,
the center which turns not,
but remains as constant
as the flow of time.
Earth, air, fire, water,
receive your own. We stint you not.
But leave us what is ours forever.

THE ASHES ARE THEN SCATTERED IN SILENCE.

Closing Words

The act is done. The words have been said.
The gate of the coming hour
now opens to us in peace.
Let us go through with thanksgiving for all that we said and did in this
    hour.
Blessed is the mystery of life and death, which is our own.
And blessed be Love forever. Amen.

SOME THINGS TO KEEP IN MIND

Whether you choose earth, air, water, fire, or a combination thereof, the committal ceremony you plan will be the most significant of your memorial rites. In a service of memory, you honor and celebrate a life—you store memories for the lonely days to come. But in the committal ceremony, you respect and begin to accept a death. Care should be taken to plan the committal and give it a ritual dimension. Some points made in earlier chapters are worth repeating:

- Give the ceremony a community context. Do not allow one person to commit ashes as a solitary gesture.

- Prepare to create sacred space and sacred time. And prepare yourself to enter sacred space and sacred time—where you will feel safe with your own emotions and will be able to be fully present. Plan to participate and involve others as much as you can.

- Mark your ceremony with a beginning and an ending. Do not be casual about what is part of the ceremony and what is not. I recommend some form of a procession, even if it is no more than a ceremonial walk from your vehicle to the committal site. If you are burying a body in a casket, consider the time-honored tradition of selecting pallbearers rather than allowing the professionals to carry the casket.

- See the committal through to its completion if you possibly can. Do not walk away from a casket before it has gone into the ground and had at least a symbolic amount of dirt shoveled into the grave. (This may require some advance negotiations with staff when the burial is in a cemetery.) In Jewish tradition, turning your back on an unburied casket is considered an affront to the dead.

- Follow the ceremony with a celebration, such as sharing food and music. Don't be afraid to ask people to bring food. It is something they can do. (People will always say, "Let me know if I can do something," which is a vague and useless offer to most grieving families. Here is a one way to put their kindness to use.)

And one more thing: Always let life have the final word. Know that your tears affirm love and that the earth that claims us all gives life and more life. Walk into day with knowledge of the night, and walk into night with knowledge of the dawn.

CHAPTER NINE

The Seasons of Grief

Rituals Through the First Year
and Beyond

My husband, chuck, received the news of his son's death on a Sunday night. After keeping some appointments on Monday morning, he caught the first available flight to North Carolina. I met him there on Tuesday evening, the funeral was Wednesday, and we took a flight back home on Thursday. Chuck missed four days of work.

That's about as much time as most people are allotted for grief in our Western culture: three days to a week. Time to "make arrangements" for a funeral or remembrance ritual and time to gather for what author Lynn Caine calls "the great memorial cocktail party."[1] Then it is expected that they will reenter the world of the living and "get back to normal." From there, they will deal with their grief privately—certainly not on company time.

Jewish tradition is an exception and offers an exemplary model for creating a calendar for moving through the stages of grief. Recognizing that people grieve much longer than three days, Judaism provides a community context for grief through time-tested practices and rituals. Those of us who are not Jewish will not derive the same meaning from traditional rituals when we appropriate them out of context, but we can certainly draw from the wisdom and practice that mark stages of grieving and create a community consciousness of the needs of those who grieve.[2]

From the moment of death to the completion of burial, the focus of Jewish rituals is on showing respect for the dead. When burial is completed, those gathered at the grave form parallel lines facing one another, and the mourners walk through this corridor of comfort. As they walk by, others recite the Hebrew words *Hamakom yenachem et'chem b'toch she'ar avelei tziyon vi'Yerushalayim,* "May the Lord comfort you among the other mourners of Zion and Jerusalem." This begins the formal period of mourning.

Jewish tradition recognizes five stages of mourning for which there are prescribed rituals. Only members of the immediate family are the mourners by obligation, but others may participate in the rituals of mourning as well.

1. *Between death and burial.* During this intense time of despair, the mourners do not receive visitors. The first full meal that they eat upon returning from the burial is called the meal of condolence. It is important that the meal is prepared by friends, not by the mourners, and conversation is discouraged while the meal is shared.

2. *The first three days following burial.* This is a time designated for weeping and lamentation; the mourners stay home.

3. *The first seven days following burial.* Called *shiva,* this is a time for receiving visitors. (This week includes the first three days, but visiting is discouraged during the first few days.) A candle or oil lamp is lit in each household where *shiva* is observed and kept burning for the entire seven days.

4. *The first thirty days following burial (includes shiva).* Mourners are encouraged to leave the house during this time and slowly rejoin society, avoiding events such as parties or entertainment.

5. *Twelve months after death.* During the next eleven months, life returns to its normal routines, but it is understood that the mourner is still wounded by the rupture of relationship that has resulted from death.

Yahrzeit marks the anniversary of the date of death. A ceremony to unveil the gravestone is conducted by or before this date.

During the periods of mourning, particularly the first thirty days, the mourners observe customs with regard to their clothing, personal habits, and religious practice. Of course, what people actually do varies according to their personal needs, the practices in their local religious community, and their level of adherence to Orthodoxy.

American culture would do well to incorporate the wisdom of Jewish practice into rites of death. Consider first the contrast between the traditional "wake" and the Jewish practice of "sitting *shiva*." A typical formal visitation period in American custom occurs prior to the memorial or funeral and lasts about two hours. It is a consolation blitz that serves more to exhaust many people than to comfort them. Their wounds are fresh, but they are expected to "hold up" through this time. If they manage to get through this occasion shedding only a few token tears, they are described as "doing well." Many take tranquilizers just to "get through it." By postponing *shiva* until after burial and marking a full week for visitation, Jewish practice provides a more sensible and sensitive context for offering comfort.

To keep a candle or oil lamp burning night and day for a full week is a simple ritual that says *this time is set aside for grieving.* Likewise, practices with regard to personal appearance, posture, and recitation of prayers all say *I am different now because I grieve.*

For those who lack the community context for marking the stages with ritual, it is certainly more difficult to set aside this kind of time. It is possible, however, to create ways to say the same thing. It is a traditional but out-of-favor custom to hang a wreath on the front door of a house where there has been a death in the family. The wreath is a way to say that the door is open to visitors. The custom of wearing black for a designated period (then gray, then mauve) has all but disappeared, but that, too, was a way of reminding people that someone in the stages of grief is in need of special caring. I know of a woman who purchased a particular piece of jewelry after her husband's death and designated it her "mourning pin." She told her family, close friends, and a few coworkers that this was her way of marking the first month as a widow. She felt that both their awareness and her own helped her through these painful days. She also wore her "mourning pin" on occasions throughout the year when she felt particularly vulnerable.

The occasions when a grieving person feels most vulnerable provide opportunities for the healing power of ritual. During the first year after a death, each birthday, anniversary, and holiday is a painful reminder of absence and loss. These occasions are also opportunities to create rituals of remembrance and mark milestones of memory.

FACING THE HOLIDAYS

For Ginny and David and their son Zeb, the winter holidays have never been the same—not since 1989, when ten-year-old Sara Jane died a few days before Thanksgiving of injuries from an automobile accident. Ginny tried to make Christmas "normal" for Zeb, who was thirteen, but as Christmas day approached, she and David knew they could not celebrate in their usual manner. Putting up stockings, for example, was too painful. How could they put up three stockings instead of four? And Ginny could not handle sitting down to Christmas dinner without Sara Jane, so she asked a friend to include them in their dinner, where Sara Jane's absence and presence were named in their expressions of gratitude and blessing. They retained their traditions for Christmas morning, which always began with a champagne toast. That year, however, and in years hence, the toast included a blessing and words of remembrance for Sara Jane.

Modifying holiday traditions is one way to mark a milestone of loss, for it says that things are different—this holiday cannot be observed in the same way. What is important is not whether you keep or change the traditions but rather that you reflect on the meaning of your holiday traditions and articulate how they are different because someone is no longer there to share what they mean. Although people have individual needs, it is wise to resist the impulse to avoid a holiday altogether.

The emotional hurdles that have to be confronted during the holidays are presented in a moving story of Jewish parents who decided they would not observe the Passover seder after their son died of a mysterious heart ailment. When the day approached, however, the mother found herself getting out the special china. As she unpacked the paper seder plate that her son had decorated in nursery school, she tearfully recalled his enthusiasm for the Passover traditions. Her husband found himself inviting a colleague to come for dinner. The guest list grew as her daughter asked if she could invite some friends. So did the dinner, which was only intended to be a "special meal," not the usual Passover seder. But a seder it was. The banished holiday they thought they would not be able to endure turned out to be a gift of grace, an evening when "grief was transmuted into sorrow"—when the ritual and its story of liberation connected the family with the larger community of friends, neighbors, and ancestors. "Why is this night different from all other nights?" said one of the children, reading from the traditional script. It was different because their child was dead; it was also different because "ancient dreams danced in the flickering candlelight, and within the ruby depths of each wineglass, bitter-sweet memories swirled."[3]

To face the first holidays after a death is to face your pain. It is to feel the deep empty ache of absence and loss. Whether you change your traditions or retain them and name your loss is not important. What matters is that you are present with yourself and one another in the pain and invite the healing power of memory into your midst.

Sometimes that healing power is in the holiday itself, for the predominant religious holidays of Western culture are about hope. Passover celebrates liberation from bondage and compassion for all who are oppressed. Easter affirms life that comes through death. The Jewish High Holy Days invite confession, purification, reconciliation, and atonement in the context of community. Thanksgiving is just that—a day set aside to give thanks. While it does not belong to any religious tradition, it honors the sacred. In the words of an ancient sage, Philo Judaeus, "The grateful soul of the wise person is the true altar of God." Gratitude heals a wounded soul. The lights of Hanukkah illuminate the dimmed recesses of the human spirit with miracles wrought by faith and love. Christmas, beneath its tinsel trimmings and commercial overlay, invites us to be present to one another and to receive the humble gift of a child of peace and love.

As grief renders the holidays more painful, the holidays can render grief less potent.

A BIRTHDAY NOT SO HAPPY

Unlike a holiday that stares you down until you have to meet its traditions and rituals with some kind of response, a birthday only reminds you that you cannot celebrate another year of a person's life. But it is a milestone of memory—an opportunity to remember well.

Sara Jane, mentioned earlier in this chapter, died in November. For her birthday in June, David and Ginny invited eight of her best friends over for a slumber party. They ate pizza and watched movies. Sara Jane's birthstone was the pearl, and each girl was given a cultured pearl necklace in her memory. Then the girls were invited to go into Sara Jane's room and choose something meaningful to them—gifts from Sara Jane that they would keep in their lives. The party mood was suspended as they all shared memories and spoke of how much they missed their friend. Then frivolity resumed as they engaged in typical ten-year-old silliness, putting on little plays and enjoying free rein of the house. At one point, Ginny noticed that one of the girls was missing. She found her in Sara Jane's room crying and just held her as they both wept. The child's mother told Ginny later that this was the first time since Sara Jane's death that the girl had cried.

Creating this birthday event was difficult, but it was an important milestone of memory. At thirteen, Sara Jane's brother, Zeb, was less able to mourn his sister's death. It was many years later that he and his girlfriend baked a cake for the occasion, blew out the candles for her years lived and unlived, and ate the cake in her honor. This simple ritual released loving and healing tears.

On the first birthday following my stepson's death, he would have been twenty-nine. My husband and I decided to begin a new tradition of donating a dollar for every year since his birth to a charitable organization. We made a ritual of writing the check for $29 and of taking it in person to the homeless shelter. We told them this was a birthday gift in honor of Tom. The following year we repeated the ritual, donating $30 to another organization.

A birthday or death anniversary may be an occasion to give away items such as clothing. The timing is an individual matter. After her husband's death, Sue Ellen was unable to let go of any of his belongings. Others urged her to give things away, especially clothing, but she held on to the objects that contained so much of him. On his birthday, she created a ritual in which she talked to him and told him that his clothing held his energy. She was going to spread his goodness back into the world. Instead of running down to Goodwill on her lunch hour, however, she set aside a "sacred time" and asked a friend to accompany her while removing the clothes and making the delivery. When she arrived at the charity she had chosen, she presented the clothing, along with a brief biographical description of her husband and a photograph of him wearing his favorite plaid shirt. She and her friend returned home to reorganize the closet, then got out the good china and had tea.

A LONELY WEDDING ANNIVERSARY

I recall speaking with a man whose wife died several months before they were scheduled to celebrate their thirty-fifth wedding anniversary. His children lived at a distance, and he became anxious and depressed as the date grew near. I asked him how they usually celebrated, and he said they would just go out to dinner and exchange gifts. Then go, I suggested. Go to dinner with some close friends. Do not spend the evening at home alone. If it is too difficult to be in a public setting, tell your friends you need to be invited to their house for dinner. He ended up going to his friends' home, where they used his wife's famous recipes for chicken divan and chocolate cake. They toasted thirty-four and a half years of a loving marriage, expressed their gratitude, and voiced their sorrow for the anniversary they could not celebrate.

The point was not to try to celebrate what could not be celebrated but to be present and cared for in loneliness and grief. And yes—to remember well.

"HALLMARK HOLIDAYS"

Even holidays like Mother's Day or Father's Day can be difficult. Like birthdays and anniversaries, they remind you of a relationship severed by death. Many people visit and decorate gravesites. Another option is to join with others who, like you, have experienced the loss of a parent or a child. Make gratitude the theme of your gathering. Invite each person to bring a candle (and holder, if needed) for each parent or child they wish to remember, and place the candles on a table. Open with a reading or a statement of what has brought you together. If you are a group of parents, ask every person or couple to light their candle and express some of the ways they are grateful they were _____'s parent for X years. If you are a group of children (including adult children), say why you are grateful that _____ was your father/mother/stepparent. Read the litany of memory (in Chapter Two or Resource Three) to close your gathering; then extinguish the candles and share a meal. You may wish to keep the candles to use for other rituals of remembering.

THE ANNIVERSARY OF A DEATH

In Jewish tradition, the word *Yahrzeit* designates the anniversary of the day a person died. It was established to honor a parent but can be observed for any relative or friend. It was not until recently that I was introduced to the *Yahrzeit* candle, which is kindled on the evening before the anniversary and burns for the entire day. A friend handed it to me a few days before the second anniversary of my stepson's death. The candle was contained in a small glass with a green and orange Manischewitz label affixed to it. "You can buy these in the grocery store," she said. "It will burn for twenty-four hours."

It burned for more like thirty hours. We lit it in the evening and chose to place it in the room where Tom had died. Oddly, both of us awoke at 1 A.M., the time of Tom's death, restless and conscious of the hour. We drew comfort from the light that flickered on the ceiling from the next room. During the day, the candle grounded us in our grief, a reminder that this day held the weight of a painful memory.

In the evening, at sunset, we invited family and friends to join us for the dedication of a small memorial stone we had selected to place in a garden corner that Tom had designed using rocks from the land. From there, we could view the pond where we had committed his ashes. We walked in a processional fashion to the location, carrying the candle and the stone. There we read the inscription on the stone, then read the litany of memory from Chapter Two, adding our own lines as we recited again and again, "We remember you." After this simple and brief ritual, we returned to the house, where we went through our photo album of Tom and talked and cried through the memories. Tom's favorite meal—pot roast with the potatoes and carrots cooked in with the meat—was on the menu for dinner.

The anniversary of a death, particularly the first anniversary, is an occasion for remembering well. Ceremonies to denote this milestone might include dedication of a stone marker, a tree, or a charitable gift made to honor a person's memory. Memorial concerts, art shows, or other events can also be presented on an anniversary as a way of offering tribute and marking the milestone.

RITUALS OF LETTING GO

Anger and guilt: at some point, almost everyone who suffers through the death of a close friend or relative comes up against these two elements of grief. As noted in earlier chapters, a memorial service can provide space to hold these feelings; therapy can help work through them. Therapists, clergy, or counselors, however, seeing the limitations of a fifty-minute session in their office, sometimes help individuals create rituals that will allow them to express and release their feelings of anger and guilt in a safe and spiritual context.

This was the case for Angela, whose father died of cancer when she was sixteen. Her family was concerned that she could not cry and asked me to talk with her. She could not really talk with me, so I suggested to her that she write a letter to her father, recalling some of the good memories and expressing her gratitude for him. A few weeks later, she sent me a copy of the letter she had written to her father. It was a very different letter than the one I had urged her to write. It was the letter she needed to write. Her agenda was not to evoke the sweet tears of memory but to open her heart and declare her sorrow that she was not more present with her father in his dying. She loved her father but could not face his illness. "Please forgive me," she wrote, "for my cruel behavior. I did not mean some of the things I said. You gave all you could to me. It meant so much; I wish I could have told you so."

She took the letter to her father's burial site and read it aloud. She was still unable to cry, but she knew that eventually the tears would come. Then, she said, she would be able to recall the memories of his love.

I was amazed at the wisdom of this teenager. Her graveside ritual did not work magic, but it gave expression to the agony in her heart. It was a first step toward getting past the feelings that prevented her from being able to remember her father well.

A ritual such as Angela performed may need to be repeated many times. Its effectiveness is also enhanced if there is at least one person present to witness it. Angela went to the gravesite alone, but she knew intuitively that she needed a witness and shared her experience with me.

Letter writing is frequently incorporated into personal rituals designed to absolve guilt or release anger. When psychotherapists work with people who are "stuck," often because of issues of guilt or anger, they sometimes help their clients craft rituals of letting go. The *components* of every ritual are the same that I have described in previous chapters: a context of community (at least one witness), sacred space (candles, scents, photos, flowers, mementos used to create a spiritually nourishing environment), and sacred time (set aside for nothing but to grieve). The *process* of every ritual will also incorporate the same basic activities: choosing a safe place and creating the space, stating your intent, going into the emotional depths, releasing or letting go of something, and then coming out and celebrating.

Rituals of letting go generally need to be *repeated many times.*

During the earlier stages of grief, creating sacred space may involve more photos or mementos—ways to keep the person present. At some point, these will be less important and can be put somewhere else.

A *spiritual context* is important. If you are going to let go of anger, to ask for strength, or to seek forgiveness, who or what do you invoke to care for your soul's secret yearnings? Where is the power of forgiveness? Where do you offer your gratitude?

In twelve-step groups, they speak of a "higher power." The process of letting go of the ability to change individuals or situations is "giving them up to the light." A ritual of letting go will be most therapeutic if you can describe the nature of your higher power, invoke its presence, and even when releasing anger is the agenda, offer gratitude. For some people, the receptive transforming power may actually be down—into the earth, mother of life. Or it may be up—into physical space, uncharted and beyond knowing. For many, an image of divine power or holy mystery is articulated in traditional terms—God, Goddess, Holy Spirit, Great Spirit, Jesus, Buddha, Kali, the Tao, and so on.

Ritual provides a structure for telling your story. Either before or during a ritual, you need a community context for relating the events or circumstances that have brought you to this place.

Writing a letter is one way to tell your story and to let go of the destructive elements of your grief. Like Angela, you may need to write it to the person who has died, expressing whatever sits heavily on your heart. The letter may need to be written to yourself, or it may be a poem or a dialogue. The words and their form are yours to create according to your need. If you wish to create a ritual of letting go but are unsure of how to shape it, it may be helpful to work with a therapist or clergy to craft something that serves your individual needs.

Recording your uncensored feelings is only part of the ritual. What you do with the poem, letter, or statement is another. I recommend going to a safe and significant location, such as a burial site, to read the letter aloud. Then what? It can be therapeutic to burn or bury the paper in a gesture of letting go. A variation on this ritual is to read the letter and burn it in one location, then put the ashes in a container and take them to a place that feels large enough to receive them, such as the ocean, a forest, or a river.

Sometimes choosing the right place is crucial to a ritual of letting go. Hendrika de Vries, a psychotherapist, was a child in Amsterdam during World War II. When she was five, her father was taken away as a prisoner to work in a forced-labor camp. During the next two years, she witnessed people starving to death and being shot in the streets. She and her mother narrowly escaped being struck by German bullets while they joined neighbors in the street to celebrate the end of the war; others fell to their death all around them. As an adult living in the United States, Hendrika tried, through twelve years of therapy, to let go of the rage and pain from those years of horror. Finally, she went back to Amsterdam, to the house where Anne Frank had lived. She stood outside the house in the rain, and it was there that she was able to weep for her lost childhood. Tears streamed down her cheeks as the rain poured over her. She suddenly realized that this cobblestone street of Amsterdam could receive her pain. The ground had held so much blood and so many tears. Yes, it could hold hers, too. She stood there a half hour or so weeping, consciously letting the earth receive her pain. Afterward, she visited an analyst she had been seeing in Amsterdam and told him her story. They celebrated with a lunch and a toast—*L'chayim!* To life!

Even when no particular anger or guilt is identified, the agony of grief may call for a ritual of release. For David, whose daughter Sara Jane was the final jewel of his life, her death in 1989 was devastating. As he saw it, he had two choices. He could die (take his own life), or he could live. Choosing to live, he asked himself, "*How* will I live? Am I going to live out the rest of my life working toward a more creative loving, healthy life, or am I going to kill myself slowly with worry, anxiety, blame, and bitterness?" He made a conscious choice for health and gathered the support he needed to do that. "You can't handle it by yourself," he tells others. "Get counseling. Join Compassionate Friends or another kind of grief support group. Your world is turned upside down. You need help. Read everything you can about grief. If you are able to walk, then walk. I didn't say exercise. Just get up, get out the door, and walk. Of course, the thing you want to do most is curl up in the fetal position and never wake up, but you need to get outside and move." David also immersed himself in the natural world, where nature teaches its lessons of death and life and rebirth, and he made allowances in his schedule for having less energy. A professional musician, he learned to play a blues instrument, the slide guitar. In a self-therapeutic morning ritual, he would play the slide guitar until the sun came up, pouring his pain into the music.

At some point, David realized that he could only go so far with therapy and healthy routines. A stubborn "wall" of anger and pain was still inside him, and he had done all he could do with talk. He needed a way to get to the primal horror and pain—to go down into the darkest place where words could not go. What helped him tear down the wall was a powerful workshop on externalizing grief in physical ways. Employing many of the same principles as ritual and making space for the kind of deep emotional release that Hendrika finally experienced in Amsterdam, the workshop allowed David to tell his story in the context of community, then to release his pain physically. The Safe Center, which sponsors the workshop, is listed among the resources at the back of this book.

Through the stages of grief, different kinds of rituals may be helpful. This was the case for a woman whose husband died in his late fifties of emphysema. She loved him deeply but was angry with him for smoking himself to death. For years, her anger intruded on her ability to remember well. She talked about her anger in her support group and with her counselor, but the ritual she needed did not develop until she had a dream in which he appeared to her young and healthy. She was shocked that he looked so good and told him, "Now you can come back because you are well."

After she had this dream, she created a dialogue with him in a session with her therapist. What emerged from the dialogue was that her husband wanted her forgiveness. She went through a series of dialogues and letter-writing rituals until she was able to forgive him. She still felt unfinished, however. Her final ritual of letting go was to sacrifice an object—something of him that she valued. The ritual of sacrifice was a conscious shift in her grieving. Earlier, she had no control over her feelings; she felt victimized by them. In her ritual of sacrifice, however, she was letting go of a part of her beloved husband that had to go on, and in making this sacrifice, she too could go on with her life. For the ritual, she used a diamond tennis bracelet he had given her for her fortieth birthday. She had one of the diamonds removed from the bracelet, and in a powerful moment of release, she threw the diamond into the ocean. Two friends witnessed her sacrifice from a distance (it was something she wanted to do alone). Afterward, they all took a walk along the shore.

FORGIVE AND REMEMBER

Forgiveness, it has been said, is giving up all hope for a better past.

In fact, it is more than that. It is inviting hope for a better future—even if the person you need to forgive is dead, and even if the person from whom you need forgiveness is dead.

Forgiveness is divine love at work in our lives. The Greek word for this kind of love is *agape.* This love is human, but it is also a transcendent power that lifts us out of ourselves. It transforms and heals, even when we are separated by time or space or death.

Forgiveness is an underused agent of healing for the symptoms of grief. There are two reasons for this. First, you cannot will yourself or anyone else to give or receive it. Second, forgiveness is entirely irrational. You can seldom find a reason to forgive or be forgiven. In fact, forgiveness is often undeserved. What it holds sacred is not fairness or justice but self-respect, spiritual health, and community.

Think about it. It cannot be controlled by human will or reason. Even the heart's choosing cannot bring about the power of forgiveness. It belongs in the realm of the Spirit, where all you can do is make yourself receptive to the healing power of the forgiveness that is a gift. And it is not even a gift from a person to a person. It is a gift of the Spirit, and we humans participate in that gift because we know that the healing within us, between us, and among us helps mend the brokenness in our world.

That is what I believe, anyway. So even when your mind and heart cannot forgive, ask for the gift. And when another person cannot forgive you, ask for the gift. And when you want to let go of a burden of guilt that you put there yourself, ask for the gift.

Anger and guilt are like the dead albatross hanging around the neck of the sailor who tells his amazing tale in Samuel Taylor Coleridge's poem, *The Rime of the Ancient Mariner*. For no reason, the mariner shot the albatross, which had flown alongside the ship, bringing the sailors a good wind. The sailors blamed him as the breeze stilled and the sails dropped, and they hung the dead albatross around his neck. After several days of stagnant calm, two hundred men cursed him one by one with their eyes and dropped dead on the deck.

The mariner was "alone, alone, all, all alone." He wanted to die but could not. In utter despair and self-hatred, he was unable even to pray. When he tried, his heart was as "dry as dust." All who were in a position to forgive him were dead. So what liberated his wretched, tortured soul was not their forgiveness.

His liberation was not in saying he was sorry or praying to God to forgive him, nor was it in cursing or punishing himself.

It was a gift. He watched the "slimy" water snakes, and a spring of love gushed from his heart, and he "blessed them unaware." That "self-same moment" he could pray; the albatross fell from his neck and "sank like lead into the sea."

The mariner received the gift of blessing in his unconscious expression of love for the slimy snakes. Just as he did not know why he killed the bird, he also did not know how he blessed the water snakes. But when his heart was as dry as dust, he knew he had severed a bond with creation, with his fellow mariners, with his God. And later, when his heart gushed with love, he knew he had reconciled. No one said, "I forgive you," or "God forgives you," but he experienced something like forgiveness through his reconciliation with the creatures of the sea. That did not mean he could forget, however, for he was wrenched with a certain agony from time to time and compelled to tell his story—over and over, again and again.

The mariner's story reflects some of the dynamics of ritual. The same healing power that freed him to bless the snakes—the same mysterious power that caused the albatross to drop from his neck—that power works through ritual. Ritual provides a structured spiritual context for the telling of story, and the more a story is told, the less power it has to evoke pain. Because a ritual declares sacred space, it invites the miracles of transformation and reconciliation. The story is told; the burden is named; the burden is released; the story is told—over and over, again and again.

The ritual is not performed so that you can forgive and forget. Rather it engages your mind, body, and spirit to forgive and remember. You know that you will never change the past, but you have a say in what happens in your life now and in the future.

The mending we do in our own grieving hearts will heal and bless us in our relationships. And it will do more than that: It will reconcile us with the holy order of the universe. It will heal and bless the world.

EPILOGUE

RICHARD AND MARK MET WITH THE RABBI AFTER STEPHEN'S DEATH. THE RABBI was explaining the process of *shiva,* which Mark and Richard planned to observe, even though they were not Jewish. As the rabbi spoke, Richard was rocking—not the sway of a person *davening* (uttering prayers in a ritual manner) but rather as a windup to an emotional explosion. All of a sudden he shouted loudly, "Rabbi, Rabbi! I know you cannot answer this question, but I want you to answer it anyway: *Where is Stephen now?*"

Undaunted by Richard's outburst, the rabbi replied, "Why, Richard, where was Stephen yesterday?"

"In the hospital, Rabbi. You know that."

"And were you with him in the hospital?"

"Of course. All day. Mark was there too."

"Twenty-four hours?"

"No, of course not. I went home to sleep."

"When you were in the hospital, did you tell Stephen how much you loved him?"

"Of course, all the time. And when I was not saying it, I felt it."

"And did you stop feeling that feeling when you were home?"

"No, of course not."

"Richard, during your entire time of being with Stephen, did you ever walk out of your own skin, step over into Stephen's skin, sit down inside him, and say, 'Oh, this is what it is like to actually be Stephen on the inside'?"

"Of course not, Rabbi. No one can do that."

"Right. No one can do that. So that means in all the years you were with Stephen, you only knew who he was within the confines of your own skin, and your own heart, right?"

"Well, yes, I guess you're right."

"Well, there inside the boundary of your skin—that is, in the loving embrace of your heart, which works the same whether Stephen appears to be near or not—that is where Stephen still is."

NOTES

CHAPTER TWO

1. Roland B. Gittelsohn, *Gates of Prayer* (London: Central Conference of American Rabbis and Union of Liberal and Progressive Synagogues, 1975), p. 552.

CHAPTER THREE

1. Matthew Fox, *Original Blessing* (Santa Fe: Bear and Company, 1983), pp. 188–200.

2. Larry Dossey, M.D., *Healing Words: The Power of Prayer and the Practice of Medicine* (San Francisco: HarperSanFrancisco, 1993).

3. Rick Fields, Peggy Taylor, Rex Weyler, Rick Ingrasci (eds.)., *Chop Wood, Carry Water: A Guide to Finding Spiritual Fulfillment in Everyday Life* (Los Angeles: Tarcher, 1984), p. 19.

4. Annie Dillard, *Teaching a Stone to Talk* (New York: Harper Colophon Books, 1983), pp. 40–41.

5. J. Donald Johnston, *Beginning Now: A Book of Explorations* (Boston: Unitarian Universalist Association, 1970), p. 47.

6. William Blake, "Eternity" *(pronouns altered).*

CHAPTER FOUR

1. Natalie Goldberg, *Long Quiet Highway* (New York: Bantam Books, 1993). Quoted passages are from pp. 217–220.

2. Lisa Carlson, *Caring for the Dead: Your Final Act of Love* (Hinesburg, VT: Upper Access Books, 1998).

3. Beth Baker, "Fighting for Funeral Rights," *AARP Bulletin,* Nov. 1999, p. 18.

CHAPTER FIVE

1. S. Hall Young, "Into the Sunset." In *Great Occasions,* ed. Carl Seaburg (Boston: Skinner House Books, 1998), p. 240.

2. Walt Whitman, "Song of Myself." In *Leaves of Grass* (New York: Hill & Wang, 1961), p. 63.

3. The words to the song, written by Joseph Bracket, are as follows:

'Tis a gift to be simple, 'tis a gift to be free,
'tis a gift to come down where we ought to be,
and when we find ourselves in the place just right,
'twill be in the valley of love and delight.
When true simplicity is gained,
To bow and to bend we shan't be ashamed.
To turn, turn will be our delight,
'till by turning, turning, we come 'round right.

CHAPTER NINE

1. Lynn Caine, *Widow* (New York: Bantam Books, 1974), p. 53.

2. Information on Jewish rituals is from Maurice Lamm, *The Jewish Way in Death and Mourning* (New York: Jonathan David, 1969).

3. Gloria Goldreich, "Different from All Other Nights." In *McCalls,* Apr. 1978, pp. 114, 208–216.

BETWEEN DEATH AND COMMITTAL

Blessing and Preparing a Body

IN *PLACES IN THE HEART*, A MOVIE STARRING SALLY FIELD, A WOMAN'S HUSBAND is shot. She finds out he is dead when neighbors deliver his body and put it on the dining room table. It's up to her to take things from there. Somehow he gets moved from the dining room into the kitchen, where the widow and her sister wash and dress his body for burial.

This was the common practice among Christians less than a century ago. In recent times, however, most funeral rites in the United States have been given over to professionals. When a person dies, even at home, professionals are called. The body is removed, and the family has no part in the preparation for burial beyond selecting clothing and delivering it to the funeral home.

There are notable exceptions, such as Jewish, Buddhist, Baha'i, and Islamic communities, where there are prescribed rituals for washing and preparing bodies for burial. Similar rituals persist in some Christian communities as well. Also, the earth-centered Pagan community and the British-based Natural Death and

Woodland Burial movement have drawn from ancient customs to develop rituals of death that provide for personal involvement.

To participate in a ritual of washing and preparing a body for burial is a way to honor a person's body with love and dignity while you bless the person's spirit. It is also a ritual of grieving and letting go.

The common element in religious rites of preparation is caring and respect for the dead. The emphasis is also on acceptance of death as a natural process. Therefore, in most of these religious traditions (especially Jewish and Muslim), a body should not be embalmed or cremated before burial.

The practices suggested here draw from several traditions and are included as examples to stimulate your thinking and research. If you plan to care for your own dead in this way, you will benefit from doing some research on the natural processes that occur in a body after death. If a person has died from a communicable disease, you should get professional help.

What you read here may help you understand your own emotional limitations as you contemplate the notion of engaging in a ritual such as this and may result in your rejection of the notion altogether. Or it may lead you to seek out funeral professionals who will help you participate, but in a less involved way. As with all of what is offered in this book, the rituals described here can be adapted and personalized according to the needs of the participants.

- The moment a person breathes his or her last breath is mysterious, awesome, and holy. It is a time to give quiet witness to the passage of a person's essence or spirit from his or her body. If you are fortunate enough to be present at the time of death, take a few deep breaths and allow yourself to be there in silence for the passage. Depending on your beliefs regarding what happens after death, this is a time to acknowledge passage into another realm. Then keep the environment serene. You may wish to dim the lighting or light a candle. If you touch the body, do so gently.

- Offer a prayer or a blessing soon after death. Depending on how many people are present, you can adapt the circle of love blessing from Chapter Three or offer a simple prayer invoking peace and freedom for the one who has died. Read a passage of scripture from your own tradition, or say something like, "May *(your word for divine or holy power)* receive you into a holy embrace; may your spirit be whole; may you be lifted on wings of love and peace into the timeless rhythms of eternity."

If you wish to wash the body, you should do it within two hours, as that is about how long it will take for rigor mortis to set in. There should be at least two people involved in the washing, clearly aware of their respective roles. Be aware that before or at the time of death, gasses or human waste may be expelled from the body orifices. Reflexive muscle spasms may occur in the limbs or facial muscles. The participants need to be able to accept these processes as well as the intimacy of washing the body. If you wish to wash or dress a body at the funeral home, you should arrange that with the staff.

- Unless it will be buried with the person, remove jewelry from the body, and offer words of blessing, particularly if you remove a significant item such as a wedding ring. Take a few moments to offer gratitude as appropriate or to name what you keep of symbolic items. If you remove a religious symbol, honor its meaning with a spoken or silent prayer.

- Remove the clothing from the body. If you wish, place a drape (preferably a lightweight naturally woven cloth) over parts of the body for modesty, and place the body on a water-resistant surface (this can be a vinyl or plastic sheet). If the person has urinated or defecated, clean the area, then cover it with cotton. You can place cotton in the rectum so that wastes do not leak, and a condom or rubber glove on the penis or cotton in the vagina. You may wish to wear rubber gloves. Keep the room as cool as possible, and keep air flowing.

- Often the eyes and mouth are open after death. If you wish, you can gently close the lids (and, if necessary, tape them closed) and, after washing, tie something around the head to close the mouth. The teeth and mouth can be cleaned, but dentures should not be removed.

- Use warm, clean water to cleanse the body, changing it as often as necessary. If you wish, add scented oils or sprigs of rosemary to your final rinse. In Muslim tradition, the body is washed twice with soap before a rinse with water and scent. A single sponge bath using water and herbs is sufficient. A small amount of alcohol can be added to close the pores.

- It is easiest to wash the body by turning it on each side. However it is done, it should be an intentional and orderly manner. For example, turn the body on the left side and wash the right side, moving from the neck to the feet. Then turn the body on the right side and repeat the procedure. Dry the body in the same intentional fashion with a clean cloth or towel. Although you may need to weep during the washing, there should be no conversation "over" the body, as your full attention should be given to the act of washing. During the ritual, you may wish to play a selection of music that feels appropriate or burn a scented candle or incense.

- The face and ears should be washed with gentle care. Hair should be washed and combed. If you wish to keep a lock of hair, wait until you have finished washing the body, then cut the hair very respectfully and put it in a designated container.

- After the body has been washed and toweled dry, you may wish to dab some scent in some body areas or to place perfumed cotton in odor-producing areas. Then dress the person in light clothing or wrap the body in clean, preferably white or natural cloth. Leave the face exposed, if you wish.

In addition to reading scripture and offering prayers or blessings from your tradition, you may wish to include other familiar rituals, such as an anointing or smudging or blessing with holy water. If clergy in your tradition are available, ask them to offer a blessing or prayer.

- You may wish to offer words of blessing as you wash parts of the body, especially the face and hands, recalling how this person has lived in this body. You can word it simply, saying things such as, "We bless your eyes, which have beheld beauty and wept with pain, which have smiled into our being; we bless your ears, which have brought music into your soul and our voices into your heart." And so on. Keeping it simple, you recall how this person has related with you, others, and with the world, through his or her body.

- Give your ritual a beginning and an ending. For example, you can begin with words of dedication, lighting a candle, or sounding a bell or chime. You can end by extinguishing the candle, offering words or a song of benediction, or repeating the sound of the bell.

FIVE SERVICES CREATED BY FAMILIES AND FRIENDS

PART OF THE INSPIRATION FOR THIS BOOK CAME FROM STORIES I HAVE HEARD from people who created their own memorial services without assistance from clergy. Each is a story of how families or extended families personalized their rituals to reflect the spirit of the person who had died. The first service was designed by and for Joni Axelrod, a young mother who died of cancer in her mid-thirties. The second service is really two ceremonies that Brad Miles created for his father-in-law, Henry, honoring Henry's passions in life in creative ways. In the third example, Janet Harvey draws on her experiences as a youth leader and hospital chaplain to suggest ways that rituals can serve the needs of teens when one of their peers dies. In the fourth service, Carey Williams, who was not involved in any religious community, describes how she incorporated and universalized meaningful rituals from her Christian background in a powerful service for her husband. The fifth service was what I call a "no services, please" memorial. It was created by Jere Jacob and her family to honor her father, Myles, who was adamantly opposed to funerals.

JONI'S GIFT

Sarah York

Perhaps the first thing to know about Joni Axelrod is that she loved children and she loved the ocean. That explains why she requested that her service be held at the beach and that the children be very, very involved. This was not asking too much. Her ten-year-old son Dylan and the children in their home-schooling group had participated in rituals of healing for Joni ever since she had been diagnosed with breast cancer. In addition to the rigorous regimen of alternative treatment she had chosen to pursue, Joni met regularly with Donna Clifton McGuire, her counselor and spiritual guide. Particularly in the last several months after Joni's cancer metastasized into her bones and she was weak and fragile, Donna also conducted several sessions during which friends and their children came together to offer her a healing presence.

I did not know Joni, but I knew Nancy, a close friend of hers who wanted me to join her, her children, and a few other families for a healing session with Joni, who was at home after four weeks in the hospital. I could feel a spiritual energy in the room where Joni, lying in the high-tech airbed that her husband, Dennis, had rented, faced windows with a view of the backyard. On a table were several sacred objects—mostly things like the rocks children had decorated for her, along with candles the children had made and fresh flowers. I had given her the "first fruits" from my rose garden a few weeks before and was moved to see the dried rose petals in a bowl on this "altar." Frail and shrunken as she was by disease, Joni was beautiful, with a radiant quality that shone through her pale skin. Her thick, long hair had been freshly brushed, and she wore a blue night-gown—blue was *her* color. She smiled with her eyes as we came in, but we could tell that she was suffering with a great deal of pain.

Part of Joni's beauty was that she was able to say what she needed and was able to receive. Several of us—adults and children—circled the bed. We sang several chants and held her in the spirit with a long and resonant *Om*. Placing our hands on her, we offered prayers and blessings. She spoke her own prayers, too.

The spiritual practices that gave Joni so much healing energy during her illness naturally became a part of the plans for her memorial at the beach. Donna opened the service with words that assured all who gathered that their level of comfort or discomfort with rituals was honored. Understanding that some people would be comfortable with things like holding hands and some would not, she stated that all who gathered were connected and gave people permission to express that in their own way. Donna wished to assure those present that there was no right or wrong expression. This was a time for them to trust the heart, free of performance anxiety. (The inherent uniqueness of the ceremony, she believes, minimizes the limiting aspects of ego and liberates spirit to guide words and actions, thus giving power to this nontraditional, participatory ritual.) Although Joni had become deeply spiritual in her last years of life, she didn't want her memorial service to be religious.

The rituals at the beach drew from those of the healing sessions. Balloons danced on the breeze, and everyone had been asked to bring a flower. These they placed in two vases as they arrived. At the end of the service, they were invited to take a flower with them. The children lit the beeswax tapers they had made themselves, and they were each given an aquamarine-colored marble—a symbol of Joni's own childlike spirit as well as her love for them.

Dennis's Aunt Laura spoke of the Jewish tradition of placing a stone on the grave. Since Joni had wanted her body cremated, there was no grave. But Dennis had selected a memorial site in the garden, where there was a special statue, and he invited everyone to select a stone from the beach and take it back to place on the statue.

The service began in the morning, and it was foggy and cold. It was also difficult to hear what people said over the sound of waves crashing on the shore. What had sounded wonderfully romantic turned out to be less than practical, and the service was moved to Joni's home, where a reception was scheduled as well.

Christyn was ten, and she had been asked to speak on behalf of the children. She had prepared her remarks, which included contributions from the other children, but she could not choke back her tears, so her mother read it for her. The children sang songs they had rehearsed for Joni, and everyone joined in singing "Wind Beneath My Wings" and other songs Joni liked, accompanied by the guitar. Several other people spoke, including Dennis, and Donna offered words of blessing.

I did not know Joni, but when I talk with those who did, it is so very apparent that she gave each one of them a gift. She had a spiritual core—a fullness of soul. But she had not always been like this. It had been during her illness, mostly through her healing meditations and sessions with Donna, that she developed her gift. Even her photographs reflected the change that others could only describe as an incredible spiritual energy. To celebrate her life was to celebrate the gift of soul that she left in the world and in the hearts of all who knew her.

HENRY'S TWO FUNERALS

Bradley R. Miles

"So what did the doctor say today, Henry?" I asked my father-in-law as he sat, relaxed, on the sofa. He was visiting us on his return from Kansas, where he had attended his seventieth high school reunion. With his thin face and tall, angular body, he sometimes reminded me of Gregory Peck in *To Kill a Mockingbird.* Even in his gaunt condition, Henry glared at me with his piercing light blue eyes. I was interrupting his Sunday weekend wrap-up news on the TV. He stayed tight-lipped, clenching a cane in his thin, bony hands. I sat silent, just looking at him, until a commercial broke his concentration.

"Not much. What was he suppose' to say?" He peered over his beaked nose. He liked to pull his "answer with a question technique." Henry was quite a conversationalist if he had control and knowledge of the subject. Politics and causes were on the top of his list, followed by family history. He considered himself a Renaissance man, but he was more of a dilettante. He never really worked long at anything unless it was something that interested him, like forging a path in the wilderness. With a few tools, a mule, and any help he could wrangle, Henry built trails in the High Sierra just so a rider could have a better vista or be able to observe a geological or historical phenomenon.

"Henry, what was your blood count? And when did you last have a transfusion?" I said in a firm tone. Henry got uncomfortable when I talked straightforwardly. To avoid being heard by my wife, Emily, and my brother-in-law, Jonathan, Henry mumbled to me.

––––––––

Bradley R. Miles lives and works on a California ranch, where he grows subtropical fruit and avocados. He has been writing short stories for seven years.

"It was a while back. The doctor knows my blood count. You go and ask him." I sat back, realizing that something was amiss.

That was Sunday. After a few phone calls on Monday, I started to understand what was happening. Between being very anemic, the travel, the stress, and getting so sick on the plane that he hardly ate, Henry's condition was not good. Tuesday morning, he went in the hospital for a transfusion and antibiotics for his infection. My wife and I talked to one of the staff nurses. "Your father-in-law says he is in a pre-leukemia, but his symptoms and lab work say different," she said. "Since you asked, I think you should talk to Hospice and weigh your options, and do it quickly. Mr. Brown's body is shutting down."

We brought Henry home to my brother-in-law's house where Henry had lived years ago, before he divorced and moved to the San Joaquin Valley to be closer to the Sierra and its trails.

I had the duty of discussing the details with Henry.

"Henry, your leukemia has advanced pretty far. Hospice is coming to help us make you more comfortable."

He glared at me, but there was no fight in him.

"I need your help on a few things, and then you can rest. Do you have a will?" I asked.

"I made one long ago, but it's lost," he answered. Henry agreed that he needed a new one, and we continued. Henry appointed me executor, power of attorney for durable health care.

"I want to be cremated, and you decide where to bury my ashes," he said one day.

"I want to be buried in a pine box," he said, out of the blue, on another day.

About three weeks after his arrival, I got a page on my beeper. Emily and I had set up a code so I knew it meant Henry had died.

When I closed the door on my truck at the ranch, everything was quiet. The front door was open. As I walked in, Emily came toward me. We hugged each other. "Henry's suffering is over," I said. I gave my other brother-in-law, Tony, an embrace.

Henry lay on his bed with Fritz, his dachshund, next to him. My son, Wesley, held Henry's hand and smoothed his hair. The ranch workers stood their customary vigilance over the bed. Henry couldn't have found a better place to die. I called the mortuary, and the workers soon came, wearing their usual dark matching suits. They loaded Henry on a gurney.

"Make sure to take him out feet first, like any cowboy would want," Tony said. That comment broke the ice. Other family members soon showed up. We sat outside and reminisced about Henry.

Before Henry died, I had worked hard to let Emily's family have time for caring and departure. I made sure Emily and her brothers took turns staying with Henry. They needed to learn to be involved in the whole process of dying. Each shift that Emily took, Wesley or our daughter, Rebekah, stayed with her. They massaged his feet or helped in whatever way to make Henry comfortable.

I left before sundown to take his dog back to Springville. Henry wanted Fritz to be with Irene, his second divorced wife. The drive at dusk gave me time to collect my thoughts and brace for the tasks ahead.

The following day, Tony went to the mortuary to sign the cremation papers. He told the undertakers not to screw around with Henry's cremation. Tony wanted Henry's every part, everything. The mortuary called a few days later, and I went to pick up Henry's effects. They gave me a plastic sack with the ashes in a cardboard box. Also included was a death certificate and a paper bag.

When I got back to my truck, I put the sack behind the seat. At the first corner, I heard a clunk. I stopped and found the paper bag partly opened. Inside were Henry's stainless steel parts to his hip replacements. For the next week whenever I took a sharp corner and heard a clunk, I turned my head and said, "Hang on, Henry."

I visited the cemetery and talked with the director, an old family friend. We arranged to put some of Henry's ashes between his two aunts who had been responsible for his coming from Kansas to California.

In my ranch shop, I made two small pine boxes using horseshoe nails to assemble them. I divided the ashes between the two boxes and then did the same with the metal hip parts. Since Henry was an avid writer, I sharpened two pencils with good erasers and put one in each box. Henry's passion for trail work was answered with two sets of pruning shears. In the lids I carved HMB.

Emily, her brothers, and her mother met me at the cemetery on a clear afternoon. We placed one of the boxes in the hole that was dug between the aunts, and made a few tearful remarks of remembrance and farewell. My brothers-in-law and I backfilled the hole and carefully replaced the cut sod.

Steven, another brother-in-law and my roommate in college, did a drawing of Henry and his dog in the Sierra looking over the Kern Canyon near the family camp. We made that into an invitation for a wake that followed the day after Henry's burial. People were invited to bring their memories of Henry to share.

The wake started with my friend, Luis, playing his guitar. He and I sang "Cielito Lindo," one of Henry's favorite songs. He liked to sing it around our campfires. I read a letter I wrote to Henry, which in part said, "Henry, you lived life to the fullest on your own terms and at your own pace. Not only did you teach me to stop and smell the wildflowers, but you taught me how to preserve them for our children." And in closing I said, "My only hope in life, Henry, is that I follow your trail, for not many a man can depart with his children at his side and be at home. I will catch up with you on that high trail beyond the Sierra."

Emily also read a letter to Henry. "Even though Mom said that Dad was happy to have a daughter, he treated me like one of the boys. He taught me how to fish, clean the fish, split firewood, cook on a wood stove, sleep in the cold, and warm up with a horse blanket. He made it clear to us that we had to take an active part in protecting our precious wilderness but to also enjoy it." Emily ended with, "Dad, I can't say that the adventures were always fun at the moment that we experienced them with you, but we sure never forgot them. And we'll never forget you. Adios, Dad. I love you—and I'll see you in camp."

Other family members spoke, then friends. Most of the recollections were of unique trips with Henry. Finally, a prayer was said, and all were invited to a fiesta at the historical society museum.

The year following Henry's death was a time for healing. Once, one of my brothers-in-law said that his children were not involved enough in their grandfather's dying. I realized that people react toward dying like animals do. If a horse comes upon a dead horse on a trail, two of his four basic thoughts come into play: fear and flight. If that same horse comes up to a dead horse that he has been pastured with for many years, fear and flight change to curiosity and despondency. People react much the same. Fear of death pushes a person away and steals that chance to act from the heart.

I knew I could not change events that were in the past, but I felt I needed to help family members who lacked a feeling of closure with Henry. Emily and I decided to bury the other box of ashes at Henry's favorite place—our family camp on the upper Kern River.

The only way to get there was by walking or riding a horse. Henry always had a special respect for anyone who made the trek to camp.

Situated on a sliver of thirty acres along the upper Kern River in the Sierra, it's located a long day's ride southwest of Mount Whitney. The drive from the valley to the trailhead is two hours on winding roads, then twenty-three miles up and down with a view at the top of the last descent into the upper Kern Canyon. After almost thirty years of riding into camp, my heart still pounds when I see the old cabins and the outdoor kitchen next to the Kern River.

The next morning, I made cowboy coffee for Wesley. That's a little coffee, lots of warm milk, and a little brown sugar. With shovels in our hands, Wesley and I walked up onto the plateau above camp.

Above the main camp on the river is a nature preserve of redwoods. Thirty-some years ago, Henry hauled the trees in on mules. The preserve was fenced with split cedar posts and rails. A canal system built by Henry and his brothers eventually ended up going through the preserve, and it kept a granite reservoir supplied with water for the camp's kitchen, cabins, and faucets. Henry loved the view from the preserve. He built benches to sit on and enjoy the vistas.

With the help of Emily and her brothers, we selected a burial spot in the preserve and found three 200-pound-size granite rocks that resembled the three peaks of Tower Rock, which loomed over the camp.

Before I left home, a local monument company sold me a carbide-tipped pointer for carving granite. By the time Steve, the artist in Emily's family, had finished incising "HMB 1913–1997," the last visitors arrived. They included ranchers, packers, rangers, teachers, and others who had a great attachment to Henry and the Sierra.

A hearty breakfast was served up. We tipped our cups, toasting Henry. The six grandchildren took turns carrying Henry's ashes up to the preserve and set them next to the hole Wesley and I had dug. The grandchildren spoke about their grandfather and how much he had taught them. I was touched by their openness and willingness to let themselves be heard. More family friends spoke, and many of the folks that rode in recalled trips with Henry in the Sierra and the lessons he gave them on geology and history. His passion for the Sierra was compared to the likes of naturalist John Muir and early Sierra Club writer Norman Clyde.

After all had been spoken, the grandchildren put Henry's box of ashes in the ground. They then filled up the hole and gave a blessing. I had asked everyone to bring a rock for Henry to start a cairn. Some of the rocks were found on the trail or taken from the Kern River. Others came from as far away as Baja California.

My brother-in-law, Tony, felt that in respect to Henry's love for fires, we should burn some dead manzanita in front of his grave. Once the fire had roared, we left it unattended, as Henry did so often, and went back to camp to eat and drink "Tower Rock specials" made of soda water from across the river and mescal and lemons from home.

On the way back to camp, one of my nieces turned to me, "Uncle Bradley," she said, "I like the services you did for Grandpa Henry. You should become a serviceman."

WHEN A TEENAGER DIES

JANET HARVEY

As one of the youth leaders in a church and as a chaplain in a major trauma center, I have witnessed and sat with the grief of teenagers and young adults. Their grief is not different from anyone else's, but it comes at a time in life when death is not supposed to happen. The capricious nature of death shatters their sense of immortality. When a friend or classmate dies or when a parent or respected adult dies early in life, teenagers and young adults have their own particular struggles and needs in the face of death. The stories of Jim, Steven, and Beth illustrate some of what teens have taught me about their special needs.

Jim

When Jim left the party, friends tried to take his keys. He and some of the others had been drinking beer all afternoon. "I'm fine," he said as he and Simon took off in the small pickup truck. Rounding a curve, they drove right into a tree. The truck caromed off the tree and rolled over into a ditch. Three hours later, Simon was in the morgue and Jim was in the emergency trauma room. Their friends found out about the accident and arrived at the hospital before any family members. Unable to get any information because they were not family members, they roamed the halls trying to find out what was happening and to support one another. Some of the hospital staff wanted them to leave. "Just go home. There is nothing you can do here. We can't tell you any-

---

Janet Harvey is a Unitarian Universalist minister, mediator, and hospital chaplain. She is also an artist, poet, and woodcrafter.

thing." They could not leave. They needed to be close to their friends, Jim and Simon. They needed to be with one another. Some of them gathered in groups of two or three—one crying and the others being supportive, one angry and the others calming him down, one sobbing and feeling totally responsible because she let Jim leave. Her friends held her and tried to let her know it wasn't her fault.

Jim's family arrived shortly before Jim died. They included his best friend, Jake, as they went into the trauma room in the emergency department to say good-bye. Later, Jake and the hospital chaplain went to the chapel where Jim and Simon's friends (and the friends of the friends) were gathered. Jake and the chaplain told them that Jim and Simon had died. No one in that moment could have understood the pain and grief like their friends.

Often youth hear about a fatal injury or death before family and will need to get together in a place where they can be with one another. A trusted adult may gather the teens at the hospital, college chapel, school, or church. They need to be together. It is too hard to go home alone with the questions, the fears, and the grief. Their friends understand and offer support in ways that parents often cannot provide.

Steven

Some of the most comforting memorial services to adult friends and relatives may not speak to the grief of teens or young adults. Youth have their own experiences with their friends that parents and other adults do not know and often do not understand. They need to shed their tears, tell their stories, play their music, and share their emotions in ways that often do not fit the services created for the families and friends of the family. Youth need to grieve and remember in their own unique ways.

Steven died just before Christmas of a drug overdose. Many of his friends were home from college visiting their families. The word went out, and other friends arrived one by one. A traditional service was planned at the church of Steven's father. Steven's friends were upset by the service. Other than mentioning Steven's name, nothing was said about who Steven was or how he had touched others' lives.

Following the service, everyone was invited to walk with the family to the outdoor chapel where Steven's ashes would be placed. After an equally dry and traditional committal, one of the mothers of Steven's friends, who had led many of them in singing, began a song that spoke to the grief and the pain that these youth felt. They began singing and the tears came. Then they began telling the stories they remembered about Steven, laughing and crying.

Later in the spring, Steven's mother held a memorial service for Steven on the Sunday closest to his birthday. This was to be a service that celebrated Steven in accord with his own spirituality and beliefs. A candle was lighted in Steven's memory by the minister who had been active while Steven was a member of the youth group at that church. Steven's drama teacher told stories about Steven the actor and student. The mothers of a number of Steven's friends provided music that they had all shared. Friends told stories of his care and concern for them as they lighted a candle to his memory. At the completion of the service, the candle lighted for Steven was extinguished, but the light of the candles of memories and wishes remained. Afterward, all were invited to have cake and ice cream in celebration of his birth.

Beth

A few months before her eighteenth birthday, Beth took her own life. The daughter of the president of the congregation, Beth was well known to almost everyone in the church. Her death shocked the adults. Beth's memorial service spoke to their questions and their concerns for the family and themselves, but her friends needed something more.

The youth were aware that Beth could be the most caring, funny, and generous friend in the world but was also deeply depressed. They had been worried about her for months. She had tried to end her life before, and they knew that. Upon notification of her death, the youth gathered at the church, and I met with them. They sat in a familiar circle with an empty space that was very naturally left for the presence of Beth. They shared their fears, their sense of responsibility and guilt, and their love for her. Together we planned a service that would take place shortly after the service in the church. Her friends decided that the service would incorporate her music and her words. It would also express our pain in her choice of leaving us so soon and our joy in her being part of our lives.

After the end of the church service, we gathered the memorial flowers according to our prearranged plan. Youth, adults, and a few children who had been very close to Beth drove to a special spot high above the Blue Ridge Parkway. We gathered in a small clearing and listened to an instrumental piece by Pink Floyd. On a cloth in the middle of our circle were placed the flowers, her picture, and objects that reminded us of Beth. We shared our thoughts, our memories, her poems, and her music, closing with Pink Floyd's "Wish You Were Here." Then we each took a flower. Finding our own special spot and saying our own personal words, we tossed the flower over the edge of the mountain.

What do youth need? Here are a few elements that are important when a young person dies:

- Time to be alone and time together with friends.
- Support in knowing what is normal in grief: numbness, loss of appetite, crying, anger, inability to concentrate, fears, strange dreams, and nightmares.
- Adults who will listen. Support people who can hold them and witness their anger and tears.
- Ways to express their grief and trusting that they will find those ways—through writing, talking, poetry, music, activity.
- Ways to incorporate their creative expressions and knowledge of their friend in a service.
- Youth closest to the deceased may need tangible objects—things that belonged to their friend that may have no meaning to an adult, such as a poster, a pin, a ticket stub to a concert, photographs, copies of poems, or drawings. They need something to hold on to, something to let go.
- If there is to be a burial, sometimes youth are invited to place special items (poems tucked in a pocket, a flower) in the casket. "Something of me goes with you, just as something of you will always remain with me."

A COMMUNION OF ALL SOULS

Carey Williams

I come from a large family of Catholics from Ohio. My parents were both very faithful to their religion, and they sent all of us kids to Catholic school until we got to high school. Although I really liked some of the nuns, I was glad when

I got to go to the public school, where it was less strict and I did not have to have my religion forced on me. When I went to college, I studied Eastern religion and philosophy and after graduation became part of an ashram connected with the Vedanta community. It was there that I met and married Ron.

During our ten years of marriage, Ron and I had two wonderful children and enjoyed our life in a small town in Virginia. After spending several years at home with the children, I went back to school, trained as a nurse, and got a job at a local hospital.

But our world fell apart when Ron, a carpenter, had an accident on the job and broke his neck. He died instantly.

As I thought about what I wanted for Ron's funeral, I talked with friends and family. We decided that we would not go to a church, partly because we did not agree on which one we might contact. Most of us wanted a Christian ceremony, but we came from different denominations. We did agree that we wanted to hold a private ceremony for family and close friends and hold a more public memorial at a later time. Since I had moved away from my Catholic religion, I was rather surprised to realize that I wanted to include some of the familiar rituals from the religion of my childhood. Even though we did not ask a priest for help, I went to a local Catholic church to light a candle and pray on my knees—something I had not done for many years. With Ron's death, I felt abandoned, angry, and unable to even think of life without him. I drew comfort from being in the house of God, where I could bring my despair and my helplessness.

We arranged with the funeral director to have a canopy and some chairs at the cemetery and planned to hold our service there. We had the chapel reserved in case of bad weather.

On the day of the service, about thirty family members gathered at the grave, which was on a lovely knoll with a view of farms and pastured hillsides. We had set up an altar near the casket. My brother-in-law James, a very good speaker, opened the service, saying some things about the shock of Ron's death and how we were there to honor his life while we sought to accept his death. Ron's sister, an Episcopalian, read a beautiful passage from the burial service in the Book of Common Prayer—from Psalm 90. Then James said:

> Let us all stand and come into a circle—a circle of love for Ron, love that he fostered in each of us, a circle of love that moves around and around and cannot be broken. We are all here today because of our love for Ron. We are here also because of our sadness at his loss. We are here to honor his life and to mark his passing. In joining hands, we join in our shared love. Please acknowledge the person to your left and to your right. It might be a squeeze of the hand or an embrace.
>
> In this time of grief, let us look to the strength of our faith. Let us each bring God into our hearts to help us heal, help us understand, help us bridge the feelings of loss and emptiness and even rage.
>
> Together now, let us say the prayer that Jesus taught. If you do not know the words, please take the words into yourself as you hear them and pray in silence. . . .

Following the prayer, James said:

> We have gathered here today, those closest to Ron, to remember, to mourn, to celebrate, and to come into a communion with his spirit. We come to honor who he was in life and in our own lives. It is through each of us that his memory stays alive and what he stood for will be carried forth.

We had decided that we wanted a communion during the service, both because it was the common ritual of our various faiths and because it was a ritual of remembering. So James said:

> On the last evening that Jesus was alive, he had a meal with his disciples, those closest to him. During the meal, he raised his cup and said, "Take this all of you and drink from it, this is the cup of my blood, the blood of the new and everlasting covenant. It will be shed for you and for all people so that your sins may be forgiven. Do this in remembrance of me."
>
> And he broke the bread, and gave thanks, and gave it to his disciples, saying, "This is my body which is given for you. Do this in remembrance of me."
>
> They gave thanks, and took the bread and the wine, and came into communion with Jesus through this simple act.
>
> People across the globe, for centuries, have reenacted this meal again and again, and we share a symbolic meal today to honor our connection to Jesus and his teachings of compassion, justice, and hope. Today, while we grieve, we also give thanks for the love that Ron has brought into our lives. As we pass the bread and the wine, taking in the love and supreme sacrifice of Jesus, let us also think of Ron. Reflect on who he was and what he brought to your life. Perhaps you will visualize him with Jesus, held in the embrace of the light and truth that is God's love.

During the communion, we sang a traditional hymn from Ron's mother's church, "Let Us Break Bread Together." It was really powerful—sharing the bread and the wine and singing the hymn. (I was not familiar with the hymn, but it was very easy to sing and quite beautiful.) There we were, a group of people from different faiths, but the ritual of sharing grounded us in the common aspects of our faith and reminded us that we were strengthened by this bond.

Then James offered a prayer, inviting us to respond, when he said "God have mercy," with the words, "Hear our prayer, O God."

> Dear God in heaven, we pray to you today. We come to you with a heavy heart—many of us not understanding why such a beautiful, loving man had to be taken so suddenly. We ask for you to be with us in our grief.
>
> *Call:* God, have mercy.
> *Response:* Hear our prayer, O God.
>
> We ask that Ron be surrounded in your love and grace as he makes his transition into the next life.
>
> *Call:* God have mercy.
> *Response:* Hear our prayer, O God.
>
> We ask for you and all of us to keep his wife, Carey, and her two daughters, Samantha and Stacey, in your thoughts.
>
> *Call:* God have mercy.
> *Response:* Hear our prayer, O God.
>
> We pray today for Ron's father, who died just ten months ago.
>
> *Call:* God have mercy.
> *Response:* Hear our prayer, O God.
>
> We open our prayers now for anyone here to add their own. Just call out your prayer as you feel moved, and we will respond with the call and the response.

Several of us offered our prayers aloud and felt heard as others responded to James's call with the response, "Hear our prayer, O God." After everyone had had an opportunity to pray, James said:

> And in closing, we pray that no one here is left alone with their grief. We pray that we can reach out to each other and help comfort and soothe the ache in our hearts.

Hear our prayer, O God. Amen.

James put his hand on the casket and said a blessing for Ron, then said:

In Jesus' death and resurrection, we are shown that death is not an end. We are born anew in spirit. Let us take a turn coming to the altar and lighting a candle in honor of Ron's bright spirit—the light within him that lives on in heaven and in each one of our hearts. As you leave, make a wish for Ron as his spirit journeys to the next place. Wish him well and say good-bye. We will leave in silence.

A "NO SERVICE, PLEASE" MEMORIAL

JERE JACOB

My father, Myles, was emphatically opposed to funerals. He thought they were largely claptrap and a terrible inconvenience, particularly for his contemporaries who were not up to traveling long distances at great personal expense just to send off an aged friend. When he died, however, my mother and I felt the need for some personal closure (I hate that locution but have not yet found a suitable alternative). Hence I came upon an idea that I felt would not offend him and would help us through the adjustment.

We wrote to all his dearest friends and relatives and asked them each, if they felt up to it, to write something about him and how he had affected their lives, particularly encouraging the irreverent approach that was his personal hallmark. We received about forty responses from contributors ranging in age from seven to ninety. I then compiled all of this into a booklet. We sent the

Jere Jacob acts in and directs plays off Broadway. She also paints houses and is very active in her eastern Long Island community.

printed book back to all the people who contributed and informed them of the day and time we had scheduled to read the book, encouraging all of them to try to do the same thing at the same time.

My mother, Peggie, and I got together with some local friends on the designated day and took turns reading aloud from the book. We laughed and wept and did all those good things one does at a wake. It worked. It could not have dishonored Myles's request, and we had our chance to "roast" him to the nines. Peggie didn't have to worry about the state of her mascara; we didn't have to prepare a meal for hundreds; and none of his eighty-something friends had to put their lives at risk traveling. We did it in the comfort of our homes. I recommend it highly. Furthermore, we all have the book at hand if we ever want to review it.

Later, on what would have been Peggie and Myles's sixtieth anniversary, Peggie and I scattered his ashes on Long Island Sound, where he used to sail in his salad days. It all felt right.

READINGS, PRAYERS, AND BLESSINGS

READINGS FROM POETRY AND PROSE

UNTITLED

A long time I have lived with you
And now we must be going
Separately to be together.
Perhaps I shall be the wind
To blur your smooth waters
So that you do not see your face too much.
Perhaps I shall be the star
To guide your uncertain wings
So that you have direction in the night.
Perhaps I shall be the fire
To separate your thoughts
So that you do not give up.

Perhaps I shall be the rain
To open up the earth
So that your seed may fall.
Perhaps I shall be the snow
To let your blossoms sleep
So that you may bloom in spring.
Perhaps I shall be the stream
To play a song on the rock
So that you are not alone.
Perhaps I shall be a new mountain
So that you always have a home.

—NANCY WOOD

UNTITLED

Hold on to what is good
even if it is
a handful of earth.
Hold on to what you believe
even if it is
a tree which stands by itself.
Hold on to what you must do
even if it is
a long way from here.
Hold on to life even when
it is easier letting go.
Hold on to my hand even when
I have gone away from you.

—NANCY WOOD

FROM **TO JOE AT HIS BURIAL**

The life contained
In your body,
Answering to gravity
And exhaustion,
Hunger and lust,
Is free;

The life you dared
To express, pursuing
Your physical edge;
The life harnessed,
As you caught and rode
On the wave of humanity,
Is free;

The life that sought
The meaning of itself,
Can now be itself;
The skin that fit you,
Weighted and held you,
Has fallen away
—Without limit, without form—;
Your spirit is now free.

We celebrate your new freedom.
We bury the shell
That held your life;
We bury the dream of you;

We bury dreams we had of you;
We bury dreams of ourselves.

We offer back to the Earth
What is hers, replacing
The remains in the depths
Of her womb.
We offer back to God
All we thought was ours,
Releasing our claims to you.

I mourn you: My life.
My spirit. My soul.
My brother. I bury
Part of myself here,
A part I imagined was me
And is not.
What separated me from you,
Has fallen away.

All that I lose
Was never mine.

What moves my legs
My heart, my breath
Will not die, or change.
This eternal me
Will remain bound to you
Forever in love,
Your sister.

—OLIVIA WOODFORD

UNTITLED

    Let me die, working.
Still tackling plans unfinished, tasks undone!
Clean to its end, swift may my race be run.
No laggard steps, no faltering, no shirking;
    Let me die, working!

    Let me die, thinking.
Let me fare forth still with an open mind,
Fresh secrets to unfold, new truths to find,
My soul undimmed, alert, no question blinking;
    Let me die, thinking.

    Let me die, giving.
The substance of life for life's enriching;
Time, things, and self on heaven converging,
No selfish thought, loving, redeeming, living;
    Let me die, giving.

                  —S. HALL YOUNG

UNTITLED

When I am gone, I shall go before you.
Think of me not as a disconsolate lover.
Think of the joy it gave me to adore you,
Of sun and stars you helped me to discover.
And this still living part of me
Will come to sit beside you in the empty room.

Then all on earth that death has left behind
Will be the merry part of me within your mind.

—ANONYMOUS

UNTITLED

Time is too slow for those who wait; too swift
for those who fear; too long for those who grieve;
too short for those who rejoice. But for those
who live, Time is Eternity. Hours fly, flowers
die, new days new ways pass by. Love stays.

—INSCRIPTION ON A SUNDIAL AT THE
UNIVERSITY OF VIRGINIA; FROM *GREAT
OCCASIONS*, CARL SEABURG, ED.

I AM NOT THERE

Do not stand at my grave
and weep.
I am not there.
I do not sleep. I am a thousand winds
that blow.
I am the diamond glints
on snow.
I am the sunlight
on ripened grain.
I am the gentle
autumn rain.
When you awaken
in the morning's hush,

I am the swift uplifting rush
of quiet birds
in circled flight.
I am the soft stars
that shine at night.
Do not stand at my grave
and cry.
I am not there; I did not die.

—ANONYMOUS

WORDS AND PRAYERS FOR
MEMORIAL AND COMMITTAL SERVICES

Opening Words

We come together from the diversity of our grieving,
to gather in the warmth of this community
giving stubborn witness to our belief that
in times of sadness, there is room for laughter.
In times of darkness, there always will be light.
May we hold fast to the conviction
that what we do with our lives matters
and that a caring world is possible after all.

—M. MAUREEN KILLORAN

Opening Words for a Suicide

Life is full of suffering. To the beloved gathered here has come a grief and loss
that strains the ability to bear—to endure the enormity of it and go on.

In the midst of brokenness and broken-heartedness may we know the grace of love that sustains us—love that endures beyond death.

May there be peace and healing. May there be acceptance that _____, beloved son and husband, father and brother (daughter and wife, and so on) chose his/her healing into death.

May all who must somehow find the courage to continue in the face of the loss of his/her presence receive the grace of healing into life. May we affirm all that was good and true and generous and beautiful in the life of _____.

May we affirm the love in which he/she was conceived and nurtured and sent forth, an autonomous human being who made his/her own decisions as we all must do.

"The heart that breaks open can contain the whole world" (Joanna Macy).

Keep breathing. Trust that your heart is large enough.

We are here to mourn the loss and to celebrate the life of _____.

Let us speak together. Let us grieve together as we share memories of _____ and all that he/she meant in the lives of those here.

—BARBARA CARLSON

Prayer for an Infant Death

God of hope and grieving, we are silent in your presence.

Help us to know that every life is whole in your eyes, no dream is incomplete in your heart.

Grant that we may come before you and each other with a measure of gratitude for the gifts we have been given—for the privilege of this bitter celebration in the circle of supportive family and friends, for the possibility of healing, for the promise of the sunrise after the lengthy desperation of grief's night.

Give to *(names of parents)* the courage to continue. Grant that they may hold fast to one another in this time of sorrow and that their family and friends may find the strength to be supportive, not backing away from the intensity of grief.

Let the stories be told over and over.

Let the tears be honored as a token of caring and of love.

Let the dreams be named and not forgotten.

Let anger be in time eased into forgiveness.

Spirit of Compassion, inspire these people to hug easily and often, for it is your hand that soothes us through this human touch. Let all hopes be cherished, that they may find a new focus and in due course come to live again.

Spirit of Life and Hope, we trust that you have taken _____'s spirit to your bosom. Help now those who remain on this earth, those whose challenge it is to reconstruct their lives and begin again in love. Amen.

—M. MAUREEN KILLORAN

Prayer

Spirit of Life, and so also our Companion in times of death, be with all who gather here in their hour of sadness. Help us to recall that we come into the world in mystery and we go away the same. Give us strength to feel the blessing of connection, which goes deeper than human knowing, and hope enough to honor the gifts of life, even in these dark days.

Be with _____ and all _____'s family and friends. Save them from bitterness or hardness of heart. Keep them open to feeling the love that remains for them, ever renewing in the world. In their grief, help them to remember always the gifts and cherish the memory that came from knowing _____.

May all here present carry forward the goodness, the love, and the courage of _____, whose life and death have brought us together today. Keep _____ safe, and may those who love her/him rest assured of what is most true, that her/his goodness and her/his beauty are at rest in the healing and sustaining heart of God.

—M. MAUREEN KILLORAN

Prayer

O God of hope and healing, we gather in your presence because we don't know what to do with our hearts in this time of loss. We call you by many names. Some of us do not call to you at all, but we are here, together, on this day.

Grant that we may go from this place empowered by your strengthening presence. May the living energy of compassion open us to the healing that comes when we give ourselves permission to grieve.

Spirit of light and so also of darkness, welcome _____'s body that will soon return to the embrace of the maternal earth, and sustain his/her spirit in the joyful celebration of eternity.

Be with this family today and in the weeks to come. May they know always that no matter how great the pain, the joy that comes from loving is always worth the risk. Help them to see, in the days ahead, the adventures that lie before them, to value the freedom that comes with new beginnings, and to know that, though _____ walks beside them no longer, they are blessed forever by the legacy of his/her love.

O God who knows our every hope and fear, cradle gently the distress of all who feel so deeply the loss of this good man/woman. Touch those who through this sorrow are reminded of the cumulative losses of their lives. Grant that each of us may hold on to a shining moment of memory, that we may carry it in our hearts as a candle, to companion us in the dark. May we have faith that goodness reigns, that hope endures, and we may feel your presence in our hearts through the continuity of trust and love. Amen.

—MAUREEN KILLORAN

Extinguishing and Relighting Ritual

Begin with a candle or lamp that is already lit. Say, "Today we would honor our beloved sister/brother and spiritual kin, _____."

Say some words about the person's special relationship to the group that gathers. Then say, "We will no longer share the touch of her/his hand and the sound of her/his voice, the sight of her/his smile. We extinguish this flame to mark her/his physical death." Extinguish the flame.

"Yet the memories of her/his special character and gifts live on in our lives. Her/His beautiful spirit is indomitable. We now light a candle to symbolize her/his influence, which endures." Light the candle.

"In mystery we are born, in mystery we live, and in mystery we die."

—CAROLYN AND TOM OWEN-TOWLE

A Litany of Remembrance

In the rising of the sun and in its going down, we remember them.
In the blowing of the wind and in the chill of winter, we remember them.
In the opening of buds and in the rebirth of spring, we remember them.
In the blueness of the sky and in the warmth of summer, we remember them.
In the rustling of leaves and in the beauty of autumn, we remember them.
In the beginning of the year and when it ends, we remember them.
When we are weary and in need of strength, we remember them.
When we are lost and sick at heart, we remember them.

When we have joys we yearn to share, we remember them.
So long as we live, they too shall live, for they are now a part of us,
as we remember them.

—ROLAND B. GITTELSOHN

RECOMMENDED READING AND RESOURCES

MAKING ARRANGEMENTS FOR ĐEATH
AND PLANNING RITUALS

From Beginning to End: The Rituals of Our Lives by Robert Fulghum (Ivy Books, 1995). Fulghum combines the wisdom of his experience as a minister with his masterful ability to tell a story. To supplement the section of the book on rituals of death, Fulghum provides a list of highly recommended resources, including the next three books cited here.

Affairs in Order by Patricia Anderson (Collier/Macmillan, 1991). A complete resource guide to all matters pertaining to death and dying.

How to Embalm Your Mother-in-Law by Robert T. Hatch (Citadel Press, 1993). Contains a serious account of what happens to the human body from the time of death until burial.

The High Cost of Dying by Gregory W. Young (Prometheus Books, 1994). A guide to funeral planning.

Caring for the Dead: Your Final Act of Love by Lisa Carlson (Upper Access Books, 1998). More than a resource for the consumer, this book invites the reader to become more personally involved in caring for the body of a person who has died. A very useful feature of the book is a state-by-state description of resources and legal procedures.

In Memoriam: A Guide to Modern Funeral and Memorial Services by Edward Searl (Skinner House Books, 1993). Includes practical considerations for planning a memorial service and features a variety of nondenominational services and scripts to be used as is or adapted.

The Pagan Book of Living and Dying: Practical Rituals, Prayers, Blessings, and Meditations on Crossing Over by Starhawk (HarperSanFrancisco, 1997). Although it is presented in the context of the Pagan spiritual belief system and is most useful to those who ascribe to those beliefs, this book describes rituals that can be adapted by anyone with an earth-centered spirituality or a desire to create rituals in keeping with natural ways. It includes blessings or prayers for specific circumstances such as infant death, violent death, organ donation, washing a body, and death in the service of life.

Funeral and Memorial Societies of America (FAMSA) offers an abundance of information at its Web site, http://www.funerals.org/famsa.

WORKSHOP

Life, Loss, and Healing Workshop, sponsored by The Safe Center. In a safe environment, this three-day workshop encourages participants to explore their own deep feelings, and includes guidance through a voluntary process of externalization of feelings. Contact The Safe Center, Leanne J. Abdnor, Director, P.O. Box 611, Annandale, VA 22003; phone: (703) 642-8827; e-mail: abdnor@safecenter.com.

SOURCES FOR READINGS, PRAYERS, AND POETRY

Great Occasions: Readings for the Celebration of Birth, Coming-of-Age, Marriage, and Death, edited by Carl Seaburg (Skinner House Books, 1998). This is an outstanding resource of readings and poetry and includes a complete index of authors and subjects. A total of 451 readings center around the themes of helplessness, desolation, grief, loss, resignation, acceptance, courage, hope, memory, commemoration, love, and affirmation.

Many Winters by Nancy Wood (Doubleday, 1974). This beautiful book of prose and poetry of the Pueblos includes several selections suitable for use in funeral or memorial rituals. Reading the book to find the selections will be a healing activity in itself. Other books by Nancy Wood are also highly recommended.

THE AUTHOR

Sarah York is a writer and Unitarian Universalist minister living near Asheville, North Carolina, with her husband, Chuck Campbell. She graduated with honors from Wake Forest University (B.A.) and Duke University (M.A.T.) before entering a career as a high school English teacher. She trained for the ministry at Harvard Divinity School, where she earned the M.Div. degree and received highest distinction as a Hopkins Shareholder. During her eighteen years as a minister, she has served congregations in New York, Maryland, and California. She is the author of *Into the Wilderness,* a book of reflections and meditations for the spring and Lenten season.

INDEX

water symbolism, 131–134. *See also* Burial; Services

Community: context of, 107, 140, 145, 154; gathering in, 40–41

Components of rituals, 153

Conflict in families, 28. *See also* Family dynamics

Containers for committal, 133–134

Coping mechanisms, 38–39

Creating rituals. *See* Rituals

Cremation: burial rituals for, 4–7; ceremonies for, 61–62; committal services for, 120–121; decision making for, 60; in Jewish and Muslim traditions, 166; natural processes of death and, 59; ownership of remains, 120; participation in rituals or ceremonies for, 12–13; requests by dying person for, 58–59; rituals or ceremonies for, 61–64, 125–126; scattering of ashes on private property, 136–137; suicide after, 63

Crisis times, 43

Custodial parents, 120

Customs, 142–144, 145

D

De Vries, Hendrika, 155

Death: acceptance of, 140; accidental, 187; acknowledging circumstances of, 99–100; AIDS, 14; anniversaries of a, 150–152; before birth, 97–99; by cancer, 172–174; of children, 120; decision making for family members, 66–67; decision making about your own, 66;

fear of, 179; first year after, 145–147; of infants, 7–9, 94–99, 200–201; naming circumstances of, 27; natural processes of, 59, 61–62, 166; observing holidays after, 146–147; permission for, 47; sudden, 52; of teenagers, 82–87, 182–186; untimely, 27–28, 93–94; violent, 27–28, 57–58, 84, 90–93; wedding anniversaries after a, 149–150. *See also* Suicide

Decision making: for cremations, 60; for family members, 66–67; with sudden death, 52; about your own death, 66

Defining a holy space, 23

Dillard, Annie, 42–43

Drug addiction, 85

Drug overdoses, 184

Dying process, 177

E

Earth from birthplace, using in rituals, 7

Earth as element of rituals, 126–129

Ecclesiastes 3, 23–24

Eller-Isaacs, Rob, 41

Embalming a body, 166

Emotional issues: holidays in first year after death, 145–147; range of, 105; recording uncensored feelings, 154; resentment/guilt, 103–104; understanding your limitations, 166

Environmental implications, 129, 130

Estates, 106–108, 114–118

Estrangement: estate distribution as result of, 106–108; irreconcilable, 121–123; by

131–134; components of, 153; creating, 7, 14, 107, 145, 150; for cremation, 12–13, 61–64, 125–126; for different stages of grief, 156; dynamics of, 159; earth as element of, 126–129; examples of personally created, 13–14; of extinguishing and relighting a candle, 203; fire as element of, 131; forms of, 9, 14; healing water, 109; for letting go, 152–157; memorial, 13; with negative environmental implications, 129; personal, 122–123; planning committal ceremonies, 140–141; process of, 153; recommended reading and resources for, 205–206; of release, 155; before removal of body, 12–13; repetition of, 153; responsive reading, 31–33; of sacrifice, 157; using earth from the birthplace, 7; washing the body, 167–169; when unable to attend services, 122–123
Rosemary, 128

S
Sacred space, 107
Sacrifice, 157
Safe Center workshop, 156, 206
Saying goodbye, 55–56
Scent, 130
Schulz, Charles, 42
Scientific deists, 107
Secrets, family, 111–113. *See also* Family dynamics
Services: allowing time for tears, 34; alternatives to traditional, 17–19; avoiding religious content in, 17; choosing the leader, 16–19; for death by cancer, 172–174; elements essential to, 20; holding a space for feelings, 83–84; in a home or yard, 25; honoring a life, 173–181; inability to attend, 85–86, 122; needs not met by, 16, 107; "no-service" memorials, 191–192; nonreligious, 112, 186–191; personalizing, 17; planning, 73–74; public or private, 125; purpose of memorial, 68; readings for, 20, 21, 191–204; responsive reading, 31–33; soul sketches, 28; spoken prayer, 33–34; teenage deaths, 182–186; time frame of, 29; tributes during, 29–31; unwanted by dying person, 1–2. *See also* Committal services; Memorials
Shakers, 77
Shakespeare, 2, 80, 127
Shame, 100–102
Sharing during services, 31
Shiva, 143–144
Slighting family members, 118–119
Sorrow, 2
Soul sketches: about, 16, 28, 68–69; honoring relationships, 69–70; interviewing family and friends for, 70–73; writing, 74–79
Speakers. *See* Tributes
Spiritual contexts, 153, 159
Spiritual work, 13
Spoken prayer, 33–34
Stages of mourning or grief, 142–144
Stones for burial rites, 127